THE ART OF BIKANER

Indian Art Series

THE ART OF BIKANER

MAHAVEER SWAMI

MOSA
Museum of Sacred Art

NIYOGI BOOKS

Overseas Distribution

USA and Canada
ACC Distribution
email: sales@accdistribution.com
www.accdistribution.com

United Kingdom, Ireland, Europe and Africa
Kodansha Europe Ltd.
email: info@kodansha.eu
www.kodansha.eu

Cambodia, Burma, Laos and Thailand
Paragon Asia Co. Ltd.
email: info@paragonasia.com
www.paragonasia.com

Jointly published by

MOSA

MUSEUM OF SACRED ART

MOSA Belgium
Petite Somme 5,
6940 Septon,
Durbuy, Belgium
Tel: +32 (0) 86 43 30 22
Email: info@mosabelgium.com
Website: www.mosabelgium.com
http://www.radhadesh.com/

MOSA Italy
Via Scopeti 106/108,
San Casciano in Val di Pesa,
Florence, Italy – 50026
Tel: +39 (055) 820054
Email: info@mosaitaly.com
Website: www.mosaitaly.com
www.villavrindavana.net

NIYOGI BOOKS
D-78, Okhla Industrial Area, Phase-I
New Delhi-110 020, INDIA
Tel: 91-11-26816301, 49327000
Fax: 91-11-26810483, 26813830
email: niyogibooks@gmail.com
website: www.niyogibooksindia.com

ISBN: 978-93-83098-73-6
Publication: 2015
Reprint: 2024

Printed at: Niyogi Offset Pvt. Ltd., New Delhi, India

CONTENTS

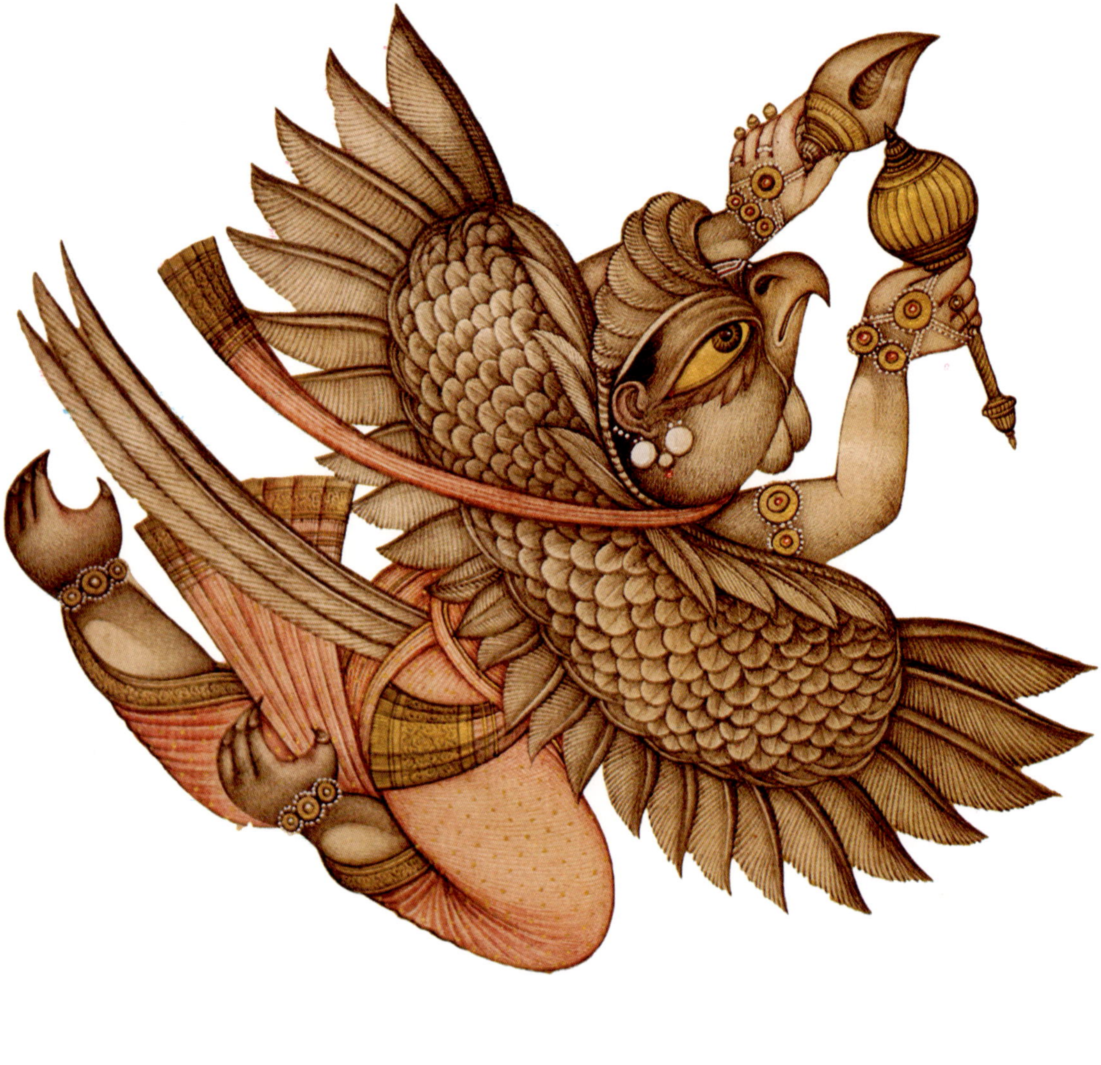

PREFACE

It is a pleasure and honor for me to present a solo show of Mahaveer Swami as one of the first temporary exhibits at MOSA. Mahaveer Swami is a well-known traditional artist from Bikaner in Rajasthan. His unique style will surely captivate the viewers who visit the show at MOSA in Radhadesh. He will surely transport them to a time long by and an India full of mystery and spirituality. Curator Sushma K. Bahl gives us an interesting analysis of Mahaveer's art which will allow the viewer to understand better the works of the artist.

India has a lot to offer to the world and its rich and varied art traditions are a good example of that. I hope Europeans will appreciate this richness. MOSA's mission is to show case traditional artists in Europe and help them preserve the traditions they are expertly representing. Mahaveer Swami is one of those artists. In India Tradition and Modernity are in permanent dialogue sometimes in harmony sometimes with tensions. We believe that they can both co-exist and enrich each other.

Martin Gurvich, Director of MOSA

Mode & Material

The artist enjoys grinding and mixing herbal medicines with stones along with specific minerals for the desired palette such as Hara Bhata (sap green) and Shilu (light green) or brunt-sienna extractable only from fossils around the river bed in West Bengal that are not available in the shops.

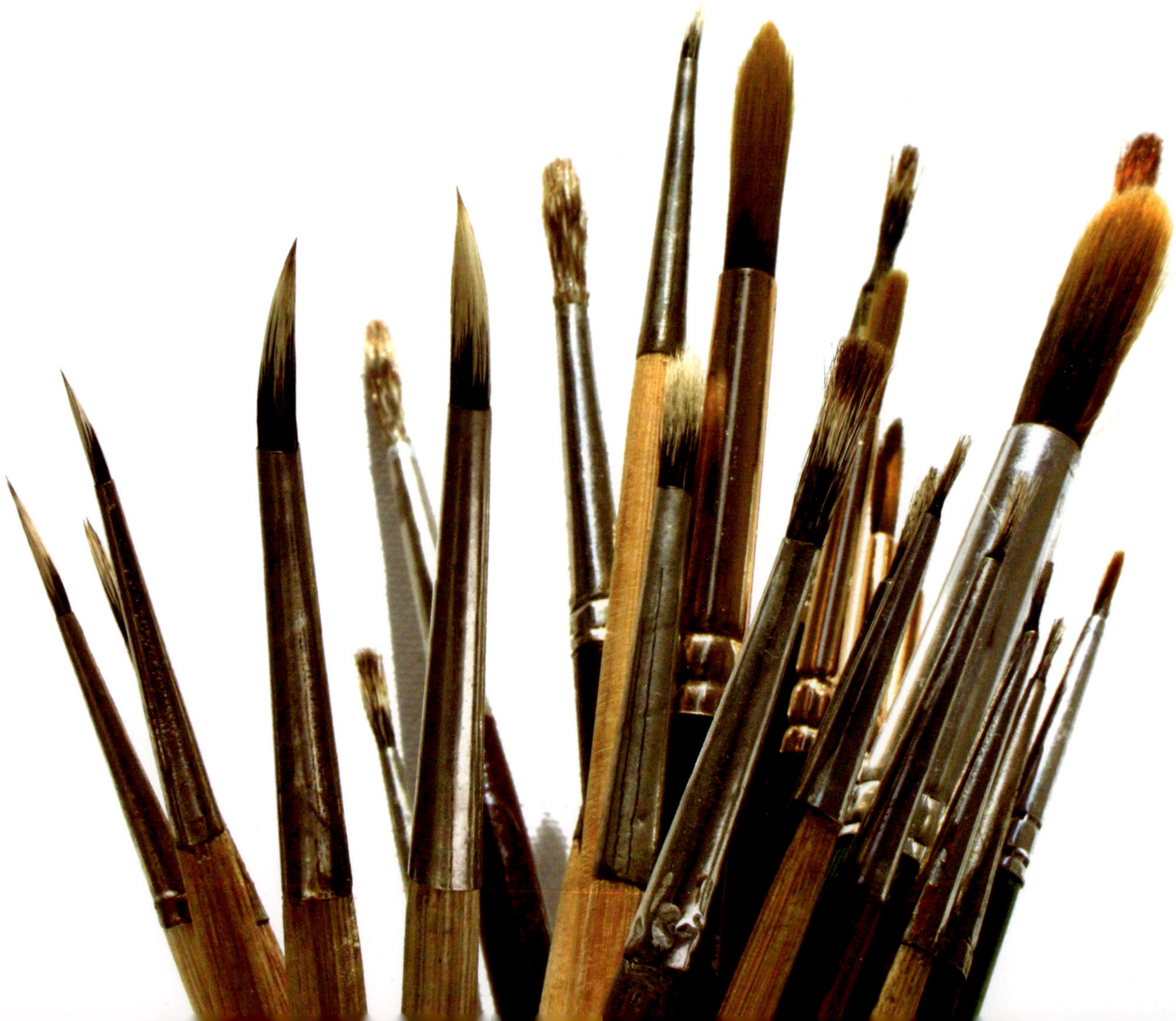

Brushes and Colours

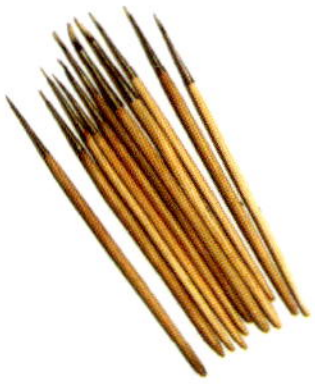

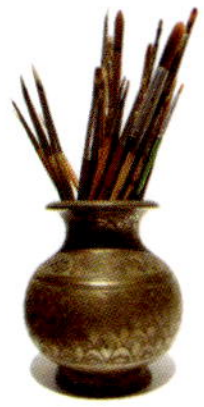

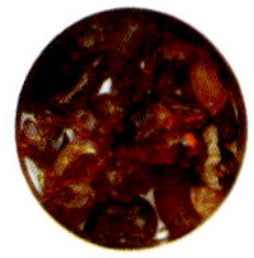

Bambol Gum
(Adhesive)

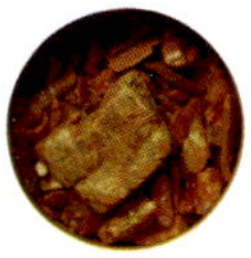

Hartal Tabki
(Yellow Colour)

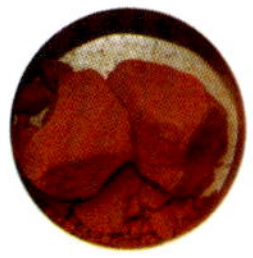

Hirmich
(Indian Red Colour)

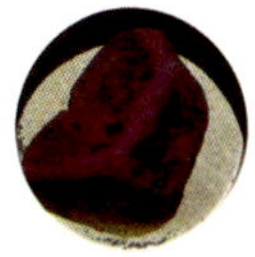

Indigo
(Blue Colour)

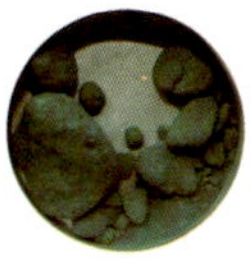

Jangal - Green Colour
(Copper Sulphate)

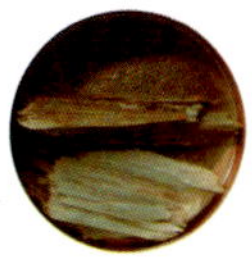

Jermora Bhata
(Light Green Colour)

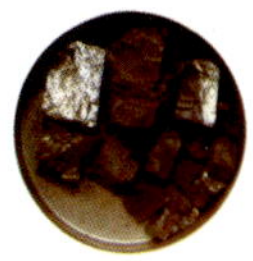

Kala Surma
(Black Mercury)

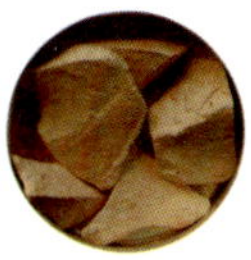

Khariya
(White Colour)

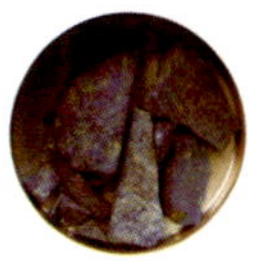

Larjward
(Lapis Lauzali)

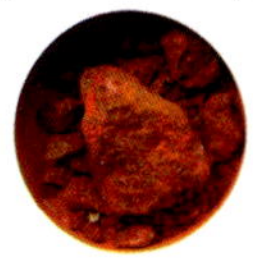

Mencil
(Orange Colour)

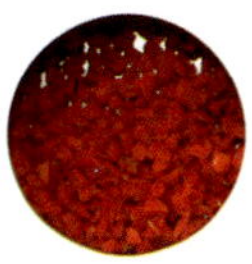

Munga - Coral Light Red
(Pink - Skin Colour)

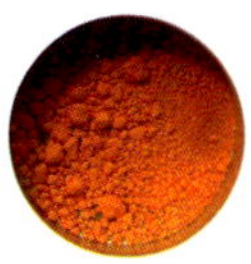

Pevari
(Deep Yellow Colour)

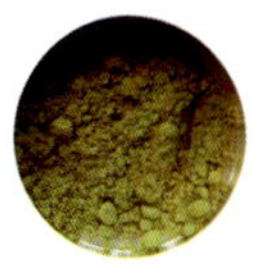

Shilu
(Light Green Colour)

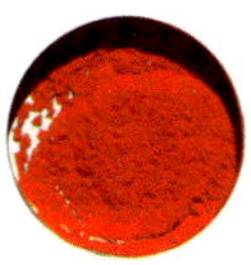

Sindur
(Bright Orange Colour)

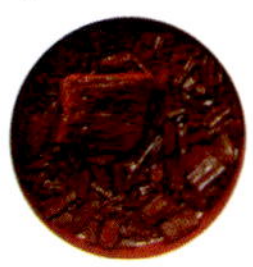

Singruf Rumi
(Crimson Red)

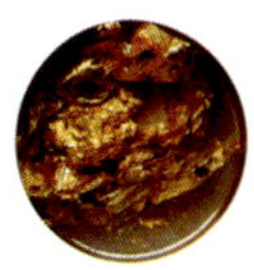

Sunhar Vark
(Gold Leaf)

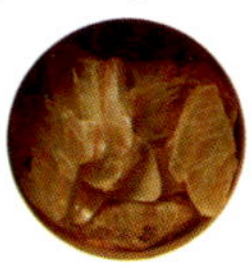

Chavladi Bhata
(White Mica)

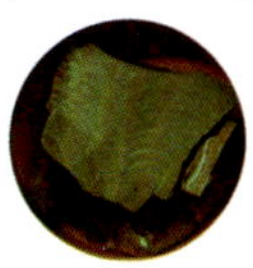

Dana Farang
(Melachite)

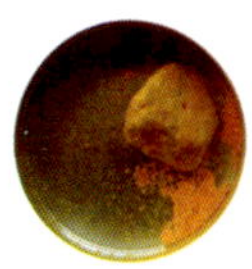

Gougali
(Yellow Colour)

The Artscape of Mahaveer Swami: Reliving the tradition of Bikaner art

By Sushma K. Bahl

The art terrain of Mahaveer Swami presents a large expanse of diverse creative reflections that mirror the artist's encounters with what he has inherited along with his response to the ever-changing time and space as in contemporary reality. In sync with established traditions and practices as exemplified in the art of illustrated manuscripts of the medieval era on the one hand, his works represent a continuum within the living arts of today's India,on the other.Incorporating decorative embellishments that draw on history and mythology, along with the surrounding habitat and abstractions from nature; his art-scape appears in a distinct and unique form and feel, coloured in the creator's own persona and passion.

ROOTS & ROUTES

Rooted in the local soil and culture of Rajasthan, the artist's creatives appear routed through his middle class upbringing in a traditional Brahmin joint family. Based in the historic city of Bikaner, he learnt to draw and paint as a child, observing first his grandfather, a chalva or mistry (head mason), make and supervise paintings on the walls of the havelis (mansions) in the desert state, and then from his father who worked in the railway workshop as a painter. Their tools, the jute bags, paper or any other left over material and colours that he could lay his hands on, kept young Mahaveer occupied for hours at a stretch. He would sit and sketch stories and scenes that he heard from his elders and draw portraits of people as observed.

And post schoolixng his fascination for art took him to Jaipur, where he trained formally at the Rajasthan School of Art. Also did a diploma in sculpture, learnt clay modeling, painting and calligraphy there. Having to fend for himself in Jaipur, the young man had to trek for miles daily and work hard on commissions making copies of paintings on pichwai, ivory and miniatures that gave him both the confidence and mastery in technique. And it was his mentor late Vedpal

Sharma Bannu ji who during the artist's internship with him, spotted his talent and advised him to focus on Bikaner style of painting.

This resulted in a change of course and Mahaveer's return to roots, creating work within the genre of Bikaner School. He made paintings on silk, canvas, paper, ivory, board and walls-whatever material was available. The rigour helped him master an understanding of the materials and tools, honing and refining his skill to work with a range of materials and in Bikaner style.

The influence of simple living and spiritual leanings on both the maternal and paternal sides; is evident in the artist's aesthetics. The studio located within an over 200 years old haveli that was gifted to his forefathers by earlier Jain inhabitants, adorns fresco work done by his grandfather. The day starts with ritual of offering prayers at the footprints of yetis, departed souls, enshrined in a little alcove within the studio. And only then begins the work. Deriving inspiration from classical scriptures of which he has a large collection, the artist sources his imagery from Indian mythology. And his understanding of minerals and organic materials that he uses in his palette comes from having observed his elders practice fresco paintings in the homes of their patrons and traditional herbal medicine that helped cure the ailing locals.

The training in making one's own paper, colours and brushes by hand has served Mahaveer well. He works mostly on wasli handmade paper, by joining two or more layers together. Given his training in calligraphy he used to sign his work in Urdu until 1982 but shifted to vernacular and English later. He has also set up a workshop/residency facility in his studio where he teaches and shares his knowledge and expertise with others including artists from Japan, Korea, and France who come to learn Bikaner style of miniature art from him. And in turn the exposure has also helped, "widen my vision to research and explore newer themes and forms ".

The form and narratives of Mahaveer's work stem from his studies of Mughal and Rajasthani miniature art traditions. The renderings reflect his command over technique acquired through rigorous discipline practiced over the years. And the life style of holy men and women, as well as mythological stories and themes that he has grown up hearing, all figure in his art. The striking profiles, meditative demeanors, expressive eyes, elaborate hair styles, impressive costumes and elegant jewelry; in ethereal colours and exquisite brushwork combined with a unique inner vision and sensitivity of the world around, are executed with finesse.

What makes his compositions more engaging is his experimentation with imagery that explores newer subjects, contexts and forms of expressions. His paintings around daily life of Indian women, a theme rarely explored by other miniature artists, bridge the gap between contemporary and traditional art. They represent the revival of the original sophistication and refinement of the Bikaner School of painting with delicate lines and tonal range associated with Mughal school pictorial quality though sans its emphasis on architectural details. Mahaveer Swami's subject matter is often drawn from the lifestyle of ascetics and mystics- sufis, pundits, saints, sages, yogis, and yoginis. He has also developed a series of paintings on Indian epics, games and festivals as well as ordinary people and their life.

MODE & MATERIAL

The artist's skill in drawing and painting, and his ability to distinguish the refined from the mundane, come from his innate understanding of the mode and materials he uses. The qualities and characteristics of the selected base material are kept in mind in planning the composition. "The ivory was washed in sea foam to rid it of oily surface, before I would begin to draw and paint". Though this medium is no longer in use, the artist has a wide choice of other material to work on, mostly handmade acid free rice paper and pure silk. He also works with equal élan on cotton, board, or wall, though paper and fine silk continue to be his preferred mode. Silk is stuck on board and paintings are made in wash technique and tempera. Chinese black ink with thin and fine brushes is applied to create shah i.e. jet-black effect and the desired texture.

Along with natural pigments such as lapis, mica, and other earth stones, that he is able to source from across the country and abroad during his travels, he uses herbal extracts, raw vegetable and other indigenous minerals and pigments that his forefathers had collected; some for fresco paintings and others for medical practice. The artist enjoys grinding and mixing the herbal medicines with stones along with specific minerals for the desired palette such as Hara Bhata (sap green) and Shilu (light green) or brunt-sienna extractable only from fossils around the river bed in West Bengal that are not available in the shops.

The minerals are preferred for the shine they exude, and organic or vegetable colours for their pristine effect. Gold, silver and blackened metal are used to add texture. Other pigments such as sindur i.e. red and yellow gougali (extract from cow urine) are used for mythological imagery."Though I can extract amazing colours from some of the stones and medicinal plants but given limited availability of such material, I also have to mix different pigments to get the right shade and also use synthetic colours now and then to get the right tone and texture", laments the artist.

The basic layout known in local parlance as Charva or stencil, done by earlier masters in thin leather sheet is planned by the artist first on paper. Shujan Khaka, the technique of working with minutely pinned holes to draw the initial sketch in black ink or pencil with fine lines, follows then. Figures are drawn and filled in subsequently with amazing range of pigments while the background is often left blank. "I enjoy playing with colours and technique", says the artist who makes a mixed use of fine pencils and slender brushes. While some of them are synthetic and bought in the market, others are handmade with squirrel hair. He credits his expertise in drawing, painting and technique of wash and tempera to his experience of commissioned work on varied base materials and textures that involved making copies of eastern- Chinese, and Korean works besides those of Jain art and in Persian style. Preferring to work in series and explore the same subject or story from different perspective, the artist has created an impressive repertoire of saints, Gods, ladies, and scenes from Mahabharata and Ramayana. Remarkable are the costumes and adornments that his characters are embellished with. His compositions also feature social customs and festivals. "I like experimenting with different styles and themes." And his botanical imagery of plants, roots, and flowers based on realistic nature studies of the flora and fauna, including the minute veins of leaves, make some remarkable compositions for their simplicity and accuracy. And birds in pairs "representing me and my wife" or in flocks to manifest the extended family and community, flying and fluttering their wings, is another recurring element in much of his imagery that make his approach to art non-academic and personalized.

Each painting goes through four stages of intensive work. Initial drawing is followed by bharai or filling in. Then follows colouring and pakai for the finish. Ghutai or rubbing is done with Akik or Agate stone on the backside of the base after each stage to make its surface smooth and allow it to soak in the colours. Embellishments are added for glow and texture work known as pardash. It takes the artist at least a week to draw and paint a single figure while the group compositions could go on for months depending on the size and details of each composition.

THE ART TRACK

The art track in this exhibition features about 60 paintings mostly on handmade paper and some on silk. Executed in Bikaner style, the works have clearly been impacted by Mughal traditions, particularly in terms of the detailed anatomical depiction, and the richness of the palette. The costumes the featured characters appear in include ghagra, choli and chuni (long skirt, shirt and stoll) for women; and men with their upturned mustache, are shown to adorn turban, embroidered sherwani (long lose overcoat) in mulmul (fine cotton) as common amongst Rajasthani Rajput folk. The detailed borders around some of the portraits and episodes painted in ornate style with finesse are reminiscent of the Mughal and Persian influence that is evident in the artist's art track in this collection.

There is an impressive collection in the art track of ascetics, priests, sufi saints, sadhus, maulvis, and pilgrims, each differently turbaned, with flowing beard, and holy markings. Lost in their meditative trance, as the artist observed them during his sojourns to Khumbh or at Ganga Sagar Math or at the famous holy Dargah shrine at Ajmer, the sketches made on site were developed into paintings working later in the studio. Incorporating elements distinct for each sect, such as Shiva devotees with three horizontal lines on forehead, with rings in ears and tiger locket as necklace, they make aesthetically delightful narratives. Particularly remarkable is the larger and multicoloured composition of a religious congregation at a camp, featuring numerous sages, and worshippers as well as their animals. Men and women representing multiple cults and sects appear engrossed in their daily routine- cooking, practicing yoga, chanting and preparing for rituals, Yagya and other devotional acts, in the painting.

Images of Radha and Krishna, inspired by Geet Govind, religious literary text, appear in a wide spread of striking compositions. The loving godly couple appears in various compositions, postures, and acts with their beautiful expressions including some, where they are featured playing Chaupad (chess like game). And there is a scene of Rukmani Harna when Krishna decided to run off and marry beautiful Rukmini. Kamdhenu, and other rituals and ceremonies; mostly in miniature format along with some paintings in slightly larger size also figure in the spread. The series on Lord Hanuman features the monkey god in various frames. Sitting atop a high pedestal of his endlessly coiled tail in one case and striding ahead holding a fluttering flag proclaiming Lord Ram, in the other.

Hanuman also appears in various other incarnations, such as carrying his famous attribute gadha or simply floating on a lotus. His playfulness is manifest in different avatars such as dancing in one, and preparing and flying kites in the others. The elephant headed lord Ganesh makes his benevolent appearance in different compositions as a family ensemble, besides enthroned atop eight distinct mounds in other compositions, and appearing with his attribute rat in a couple of works.

The repertoire also encompasses 24 distinct avatars or godly incarnations based on studies of Bhagwat puran epic as against the tradition of depicting them in ten manifestations or dasavatar, that the artist has created. Each manifestation appears with its established attributes and other distinct signifiers. And there are other mythological paintings in larger format featuring godly couples Vishnu and Lakshmi and Shiva and Parvathi as well as those featuring episodes from Ramayana and Mahabharata. The Artscape of Mahaveer Swami, brings alive the richness in the art tradition of Bikaner. Inspired by his religious and artistic upbringing, along with his rigorous training, and now suitably supported by his young son Anurag, a trained and accomplished artist himself, Mahaveer is able to take forward his ideas and work into newer arenas. The elaborate background, distinct elements and facial expressions in each of his work add up to make his art dynamic and aesthetically distinct. Marked for their sophistication, the artistic renderings in the collection resonate with an inextricable intertwining between art and life that has won the artist several honours and exhibitions, besides publication and documentation in books.

Author of 5000 Years of Indian Art, *and former Head, Arts & Culture, British Council India, Sushma K. Bahl MBE, is an independent arts adviser, writer and curator of cultural projects, based in Delhi. Guest Director for XI Triennale-India 2005, Project Consultant for Bharat Rang Mahotsav X11, and Jury Member for the 14th Asian Art Biennale Bangladesh 2010, curator of India- ASEAN artists' residency & exhibition in 2012 amongst other projects;* Ways of Seeing *won her the best-curated group show IHC Art India Award. Editor and contributor for catalogs and artists' books including those on Thota Vaikuntam, Paresh Maity, Satish Gupta, Sarla Chandra, and Shuvaprasanna, Sushma Bahl is a trustee and advisory board member of a select few cultural institutions in India and abroad.*

GEET GOVINDA

Radha and Krishna >
Natural pigments on handmade paper, 23x16cm

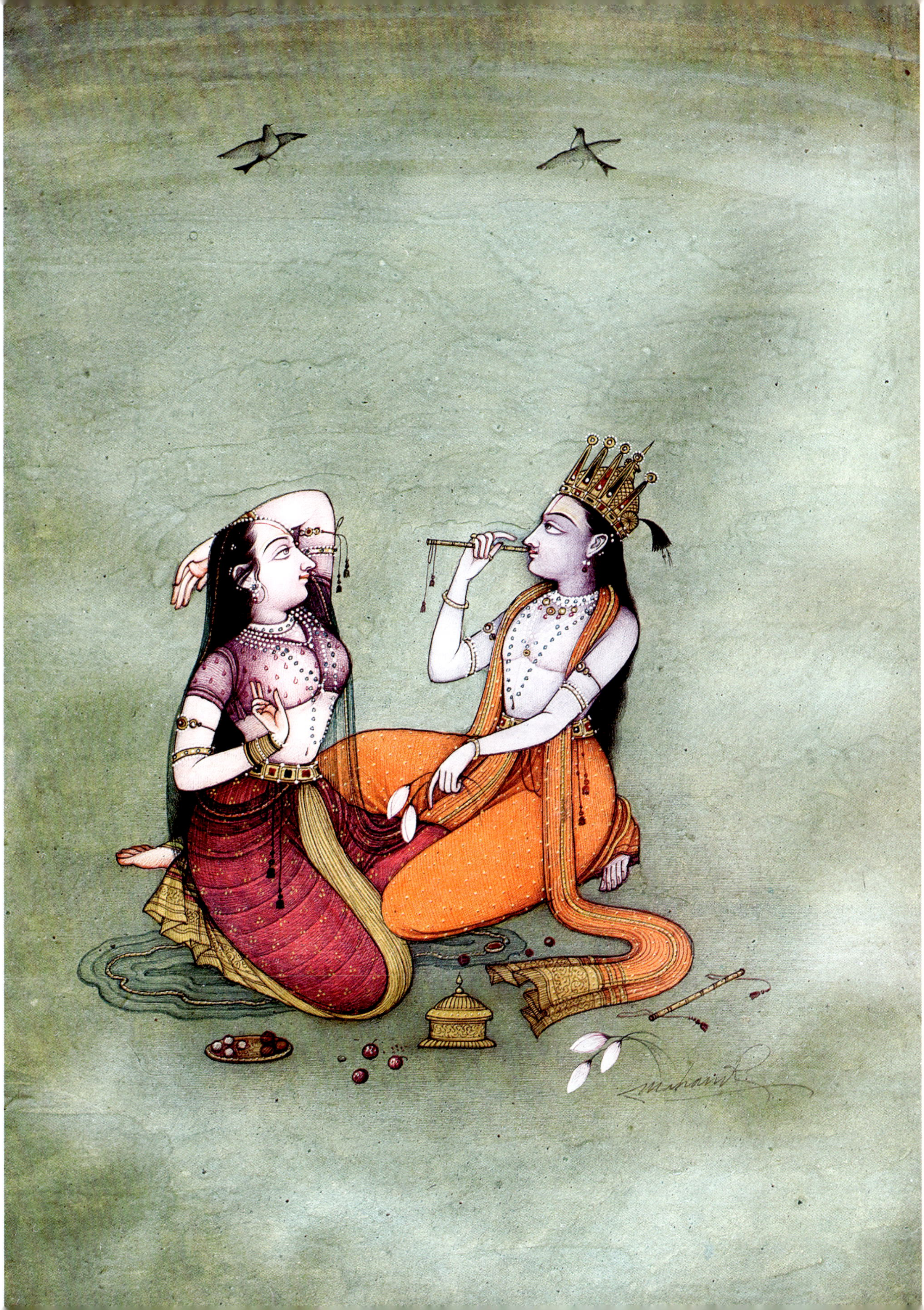

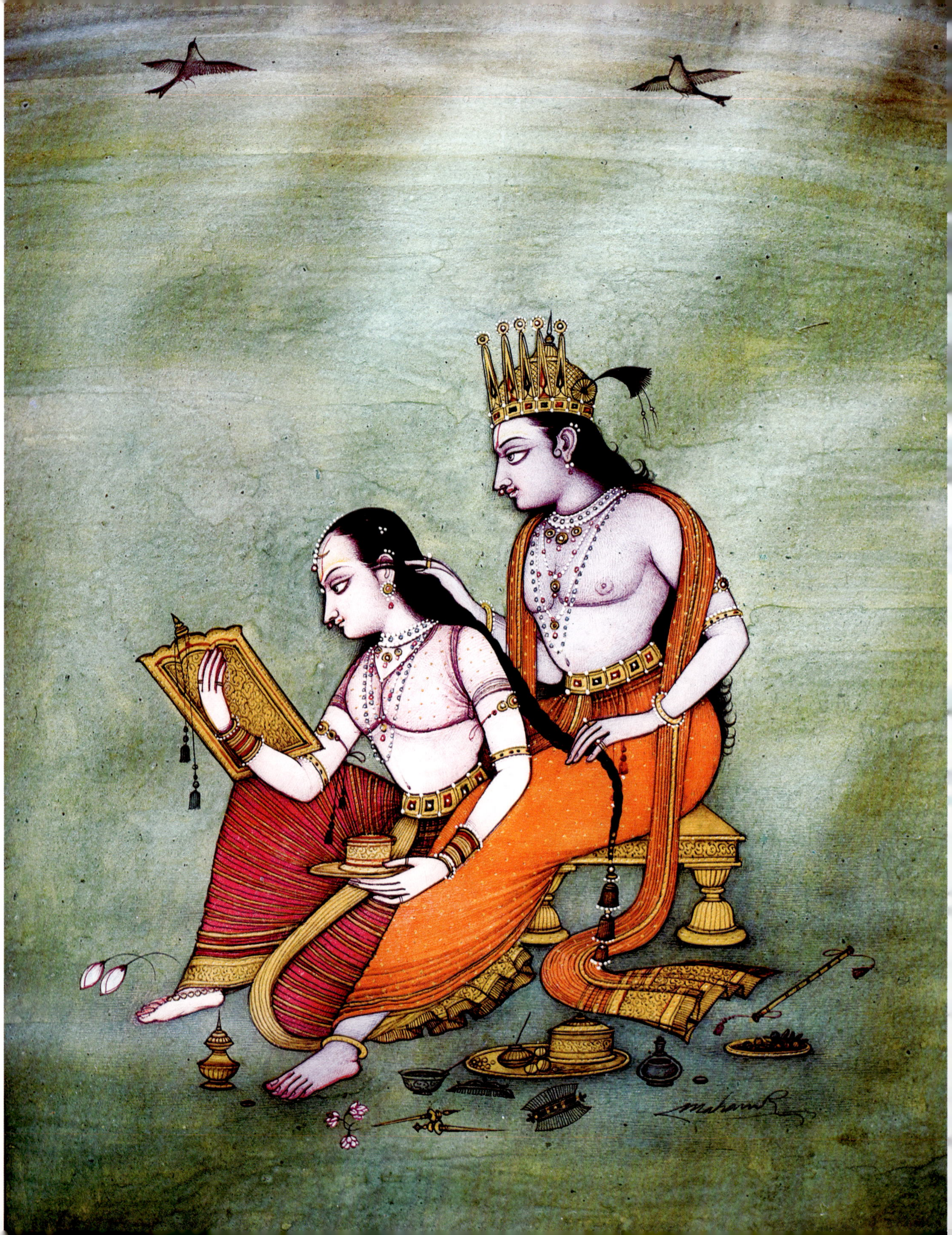

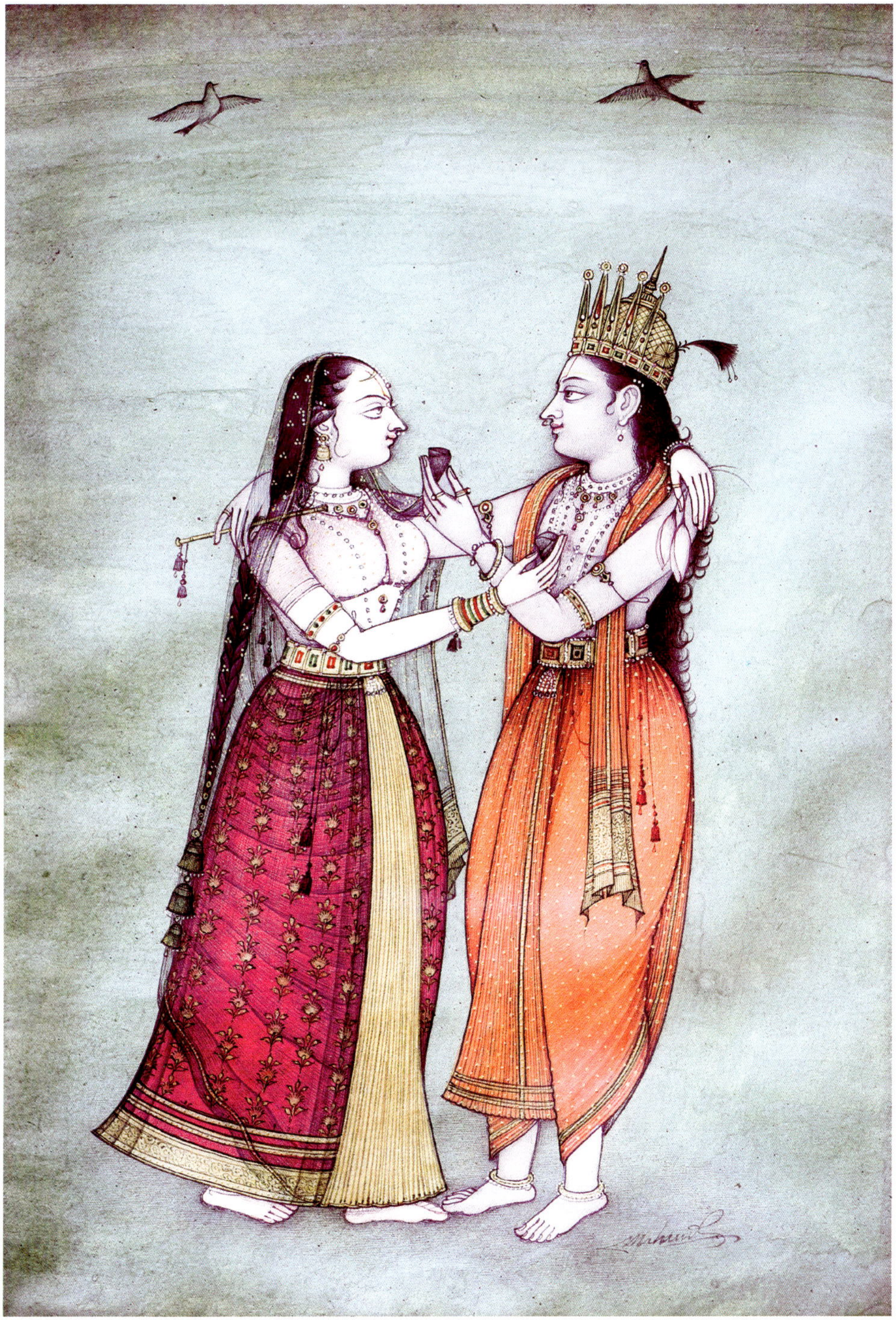

< Radha and Krishna
Natural pigments on handmade paper, 23x16cm

∧ Radha and Krishna
Natural pigments on handmade paper, 23x16cm

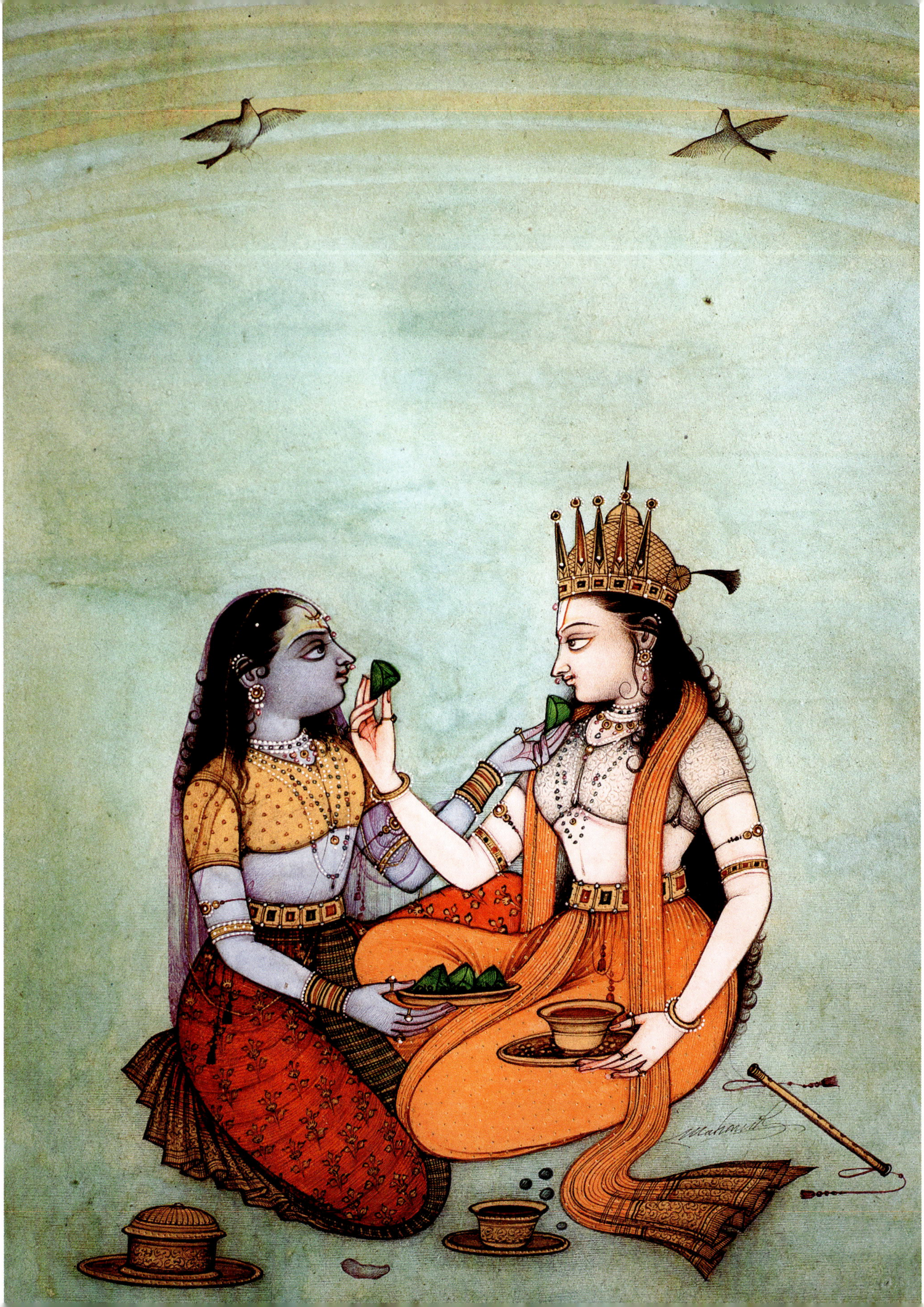

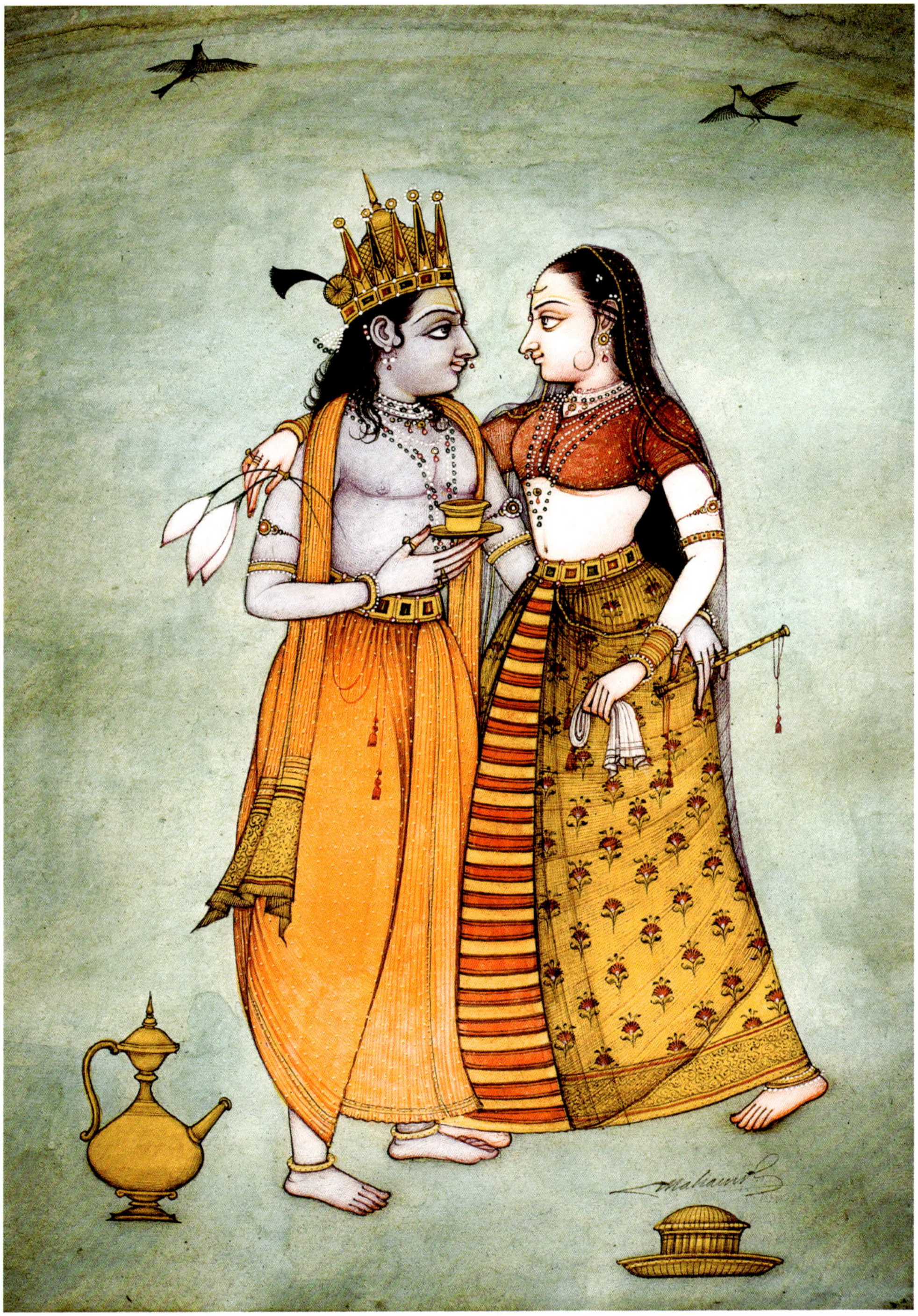

< Radha and Krishna
Natural pigments on handmade paper, 23x16cm

∧ Radha and Krishna
Natural pigments on handmade paper, 23x16cm

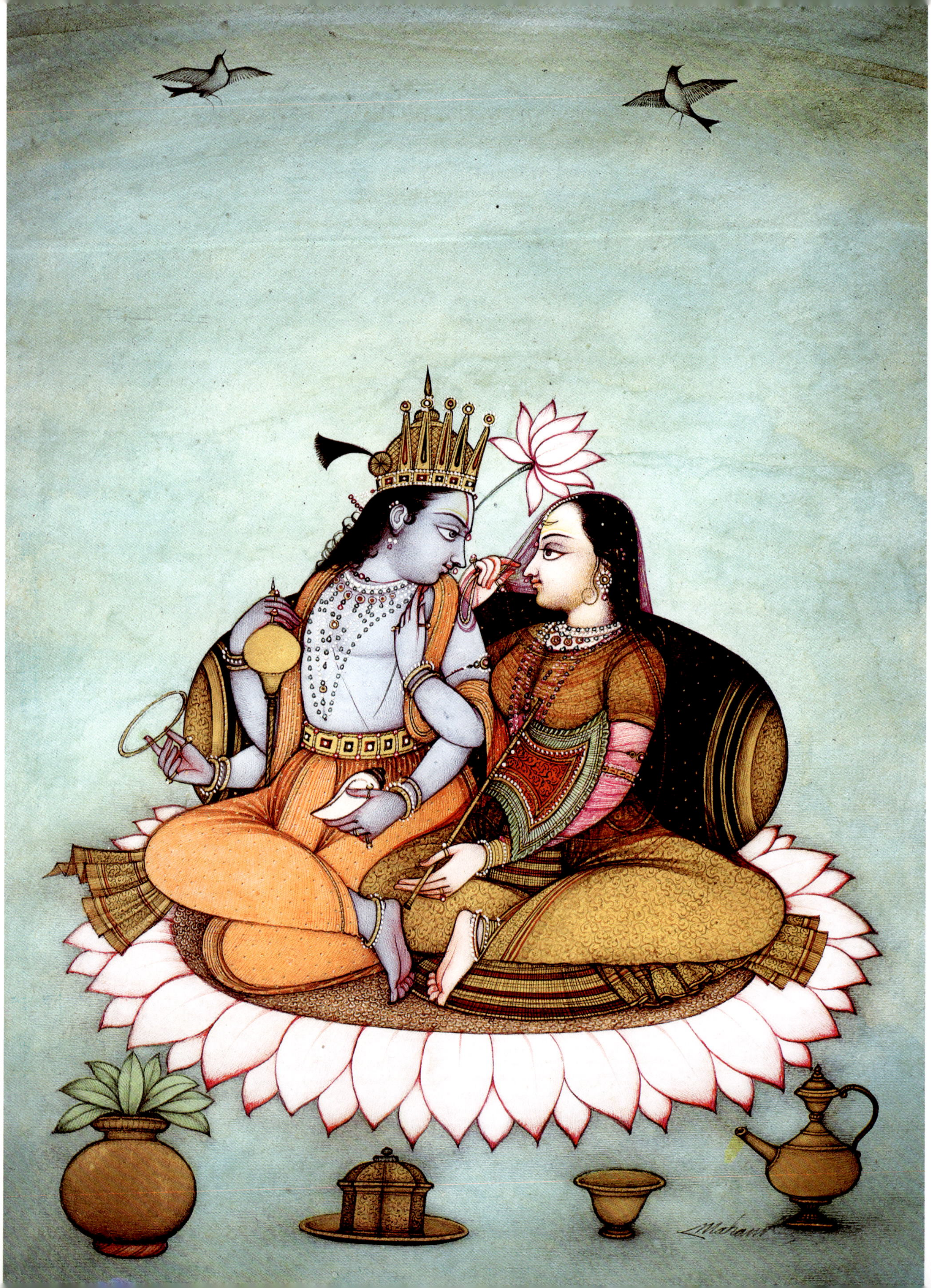

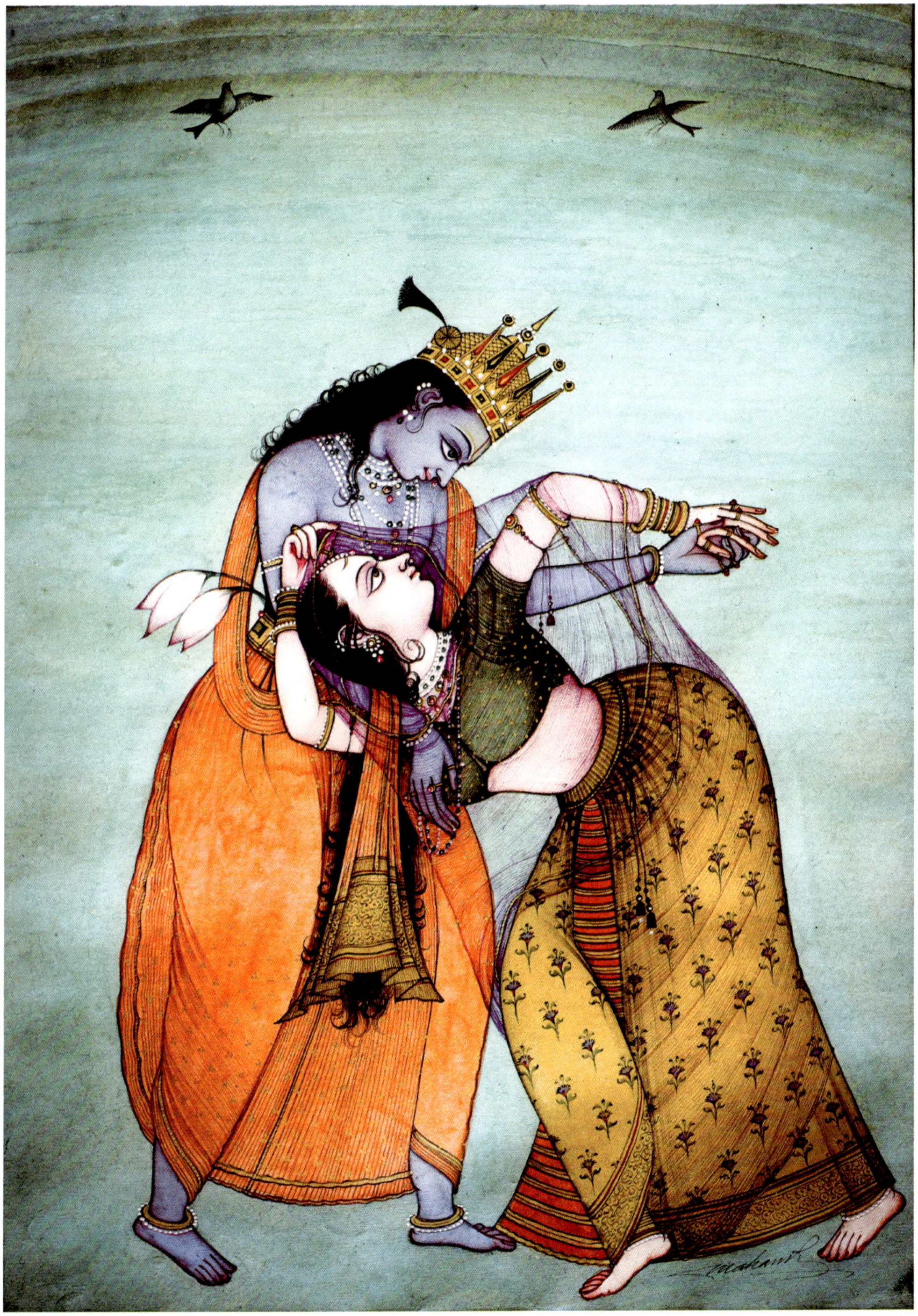

< Radha and Krishna
Natural pigments on handmade paper, 23x16cm

∧ Radha and Krishna
Natural pigments on handmade paper, 23x16cm

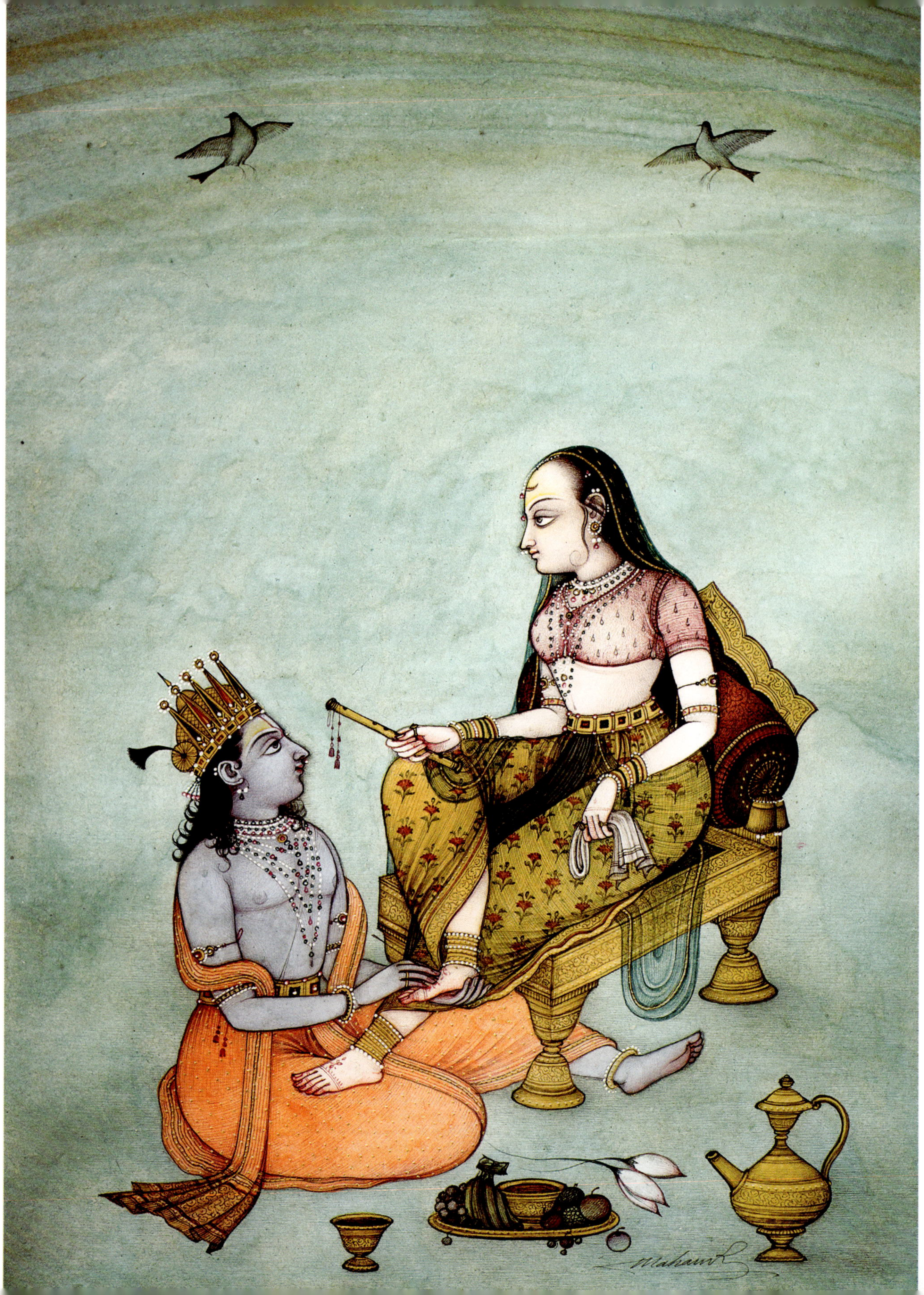

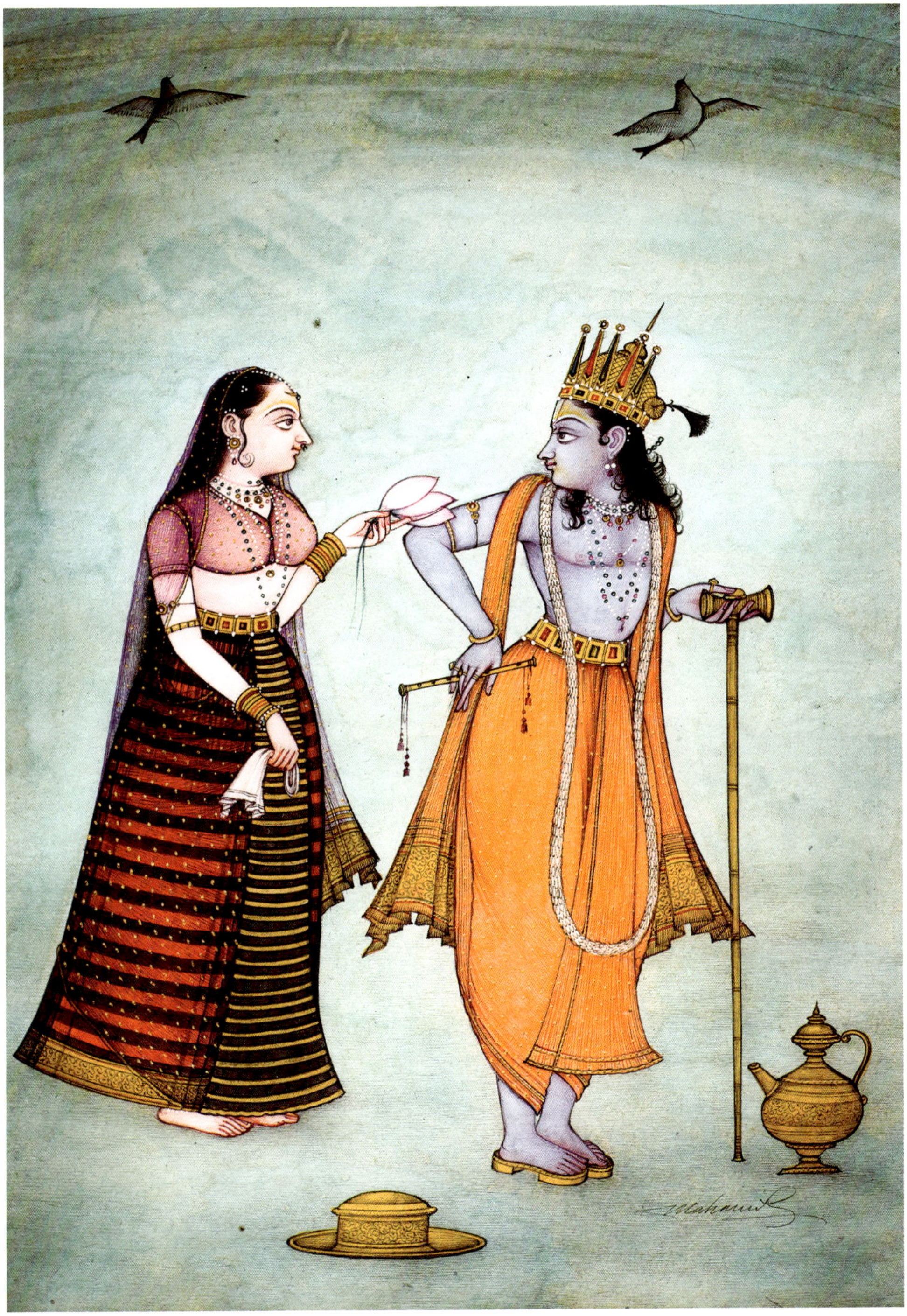

< Radha and Krishna
Natural pigments on handmade paper, 23x16cm

∧ Radha and Krishna
Natural pigments on handmade paper, 23x16cm

SADHUS

Sadhu >
Natural pigments on handmade paper, 23x13cm

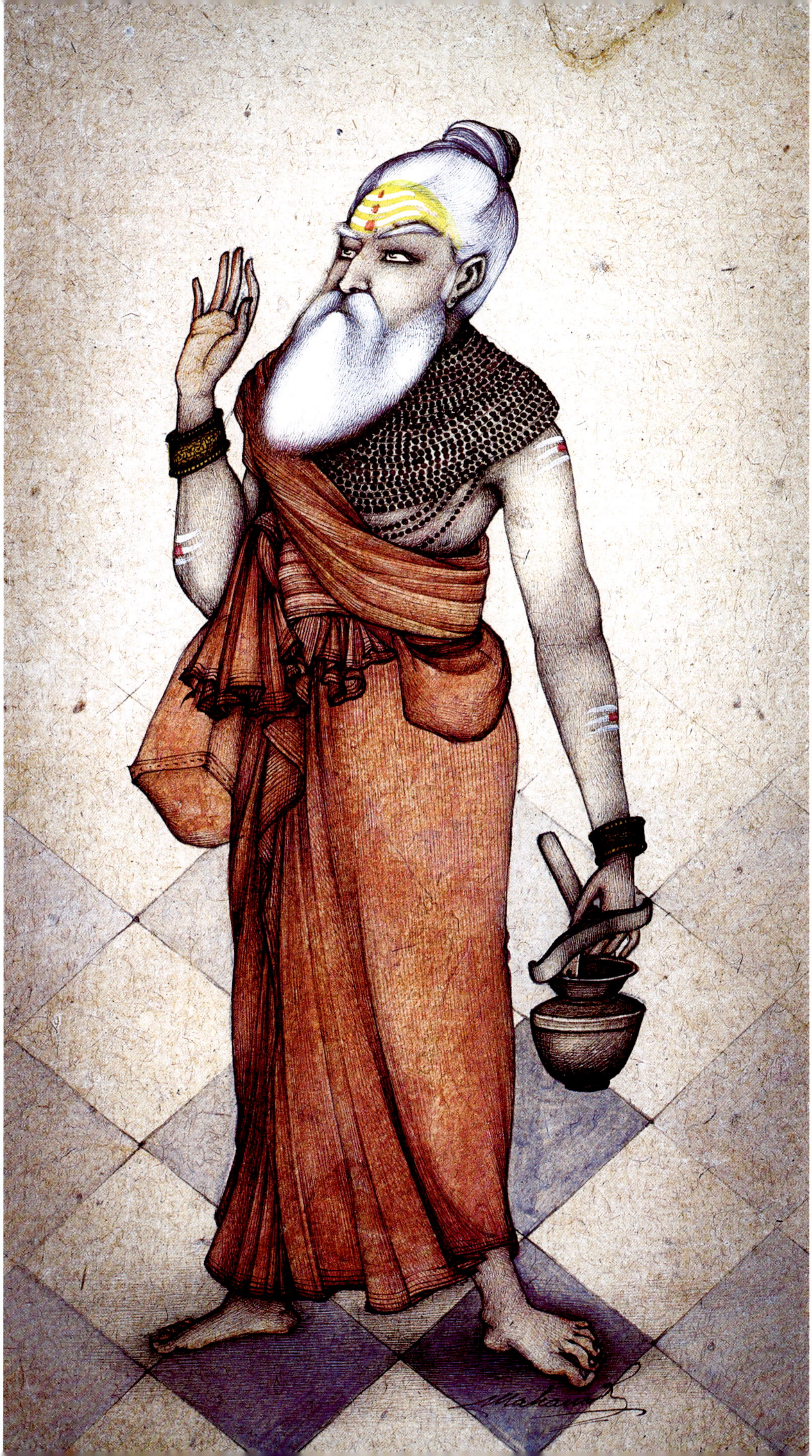

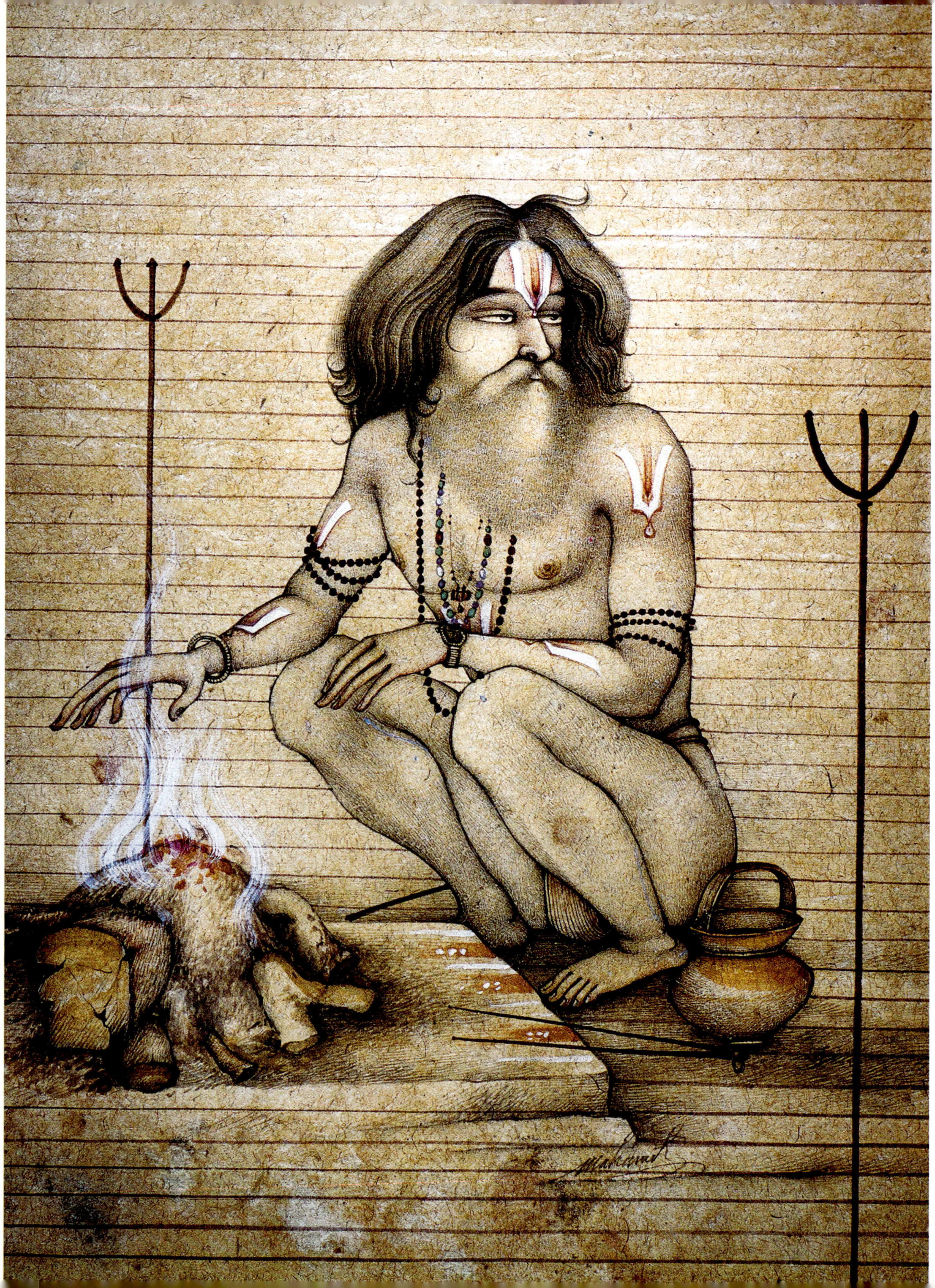

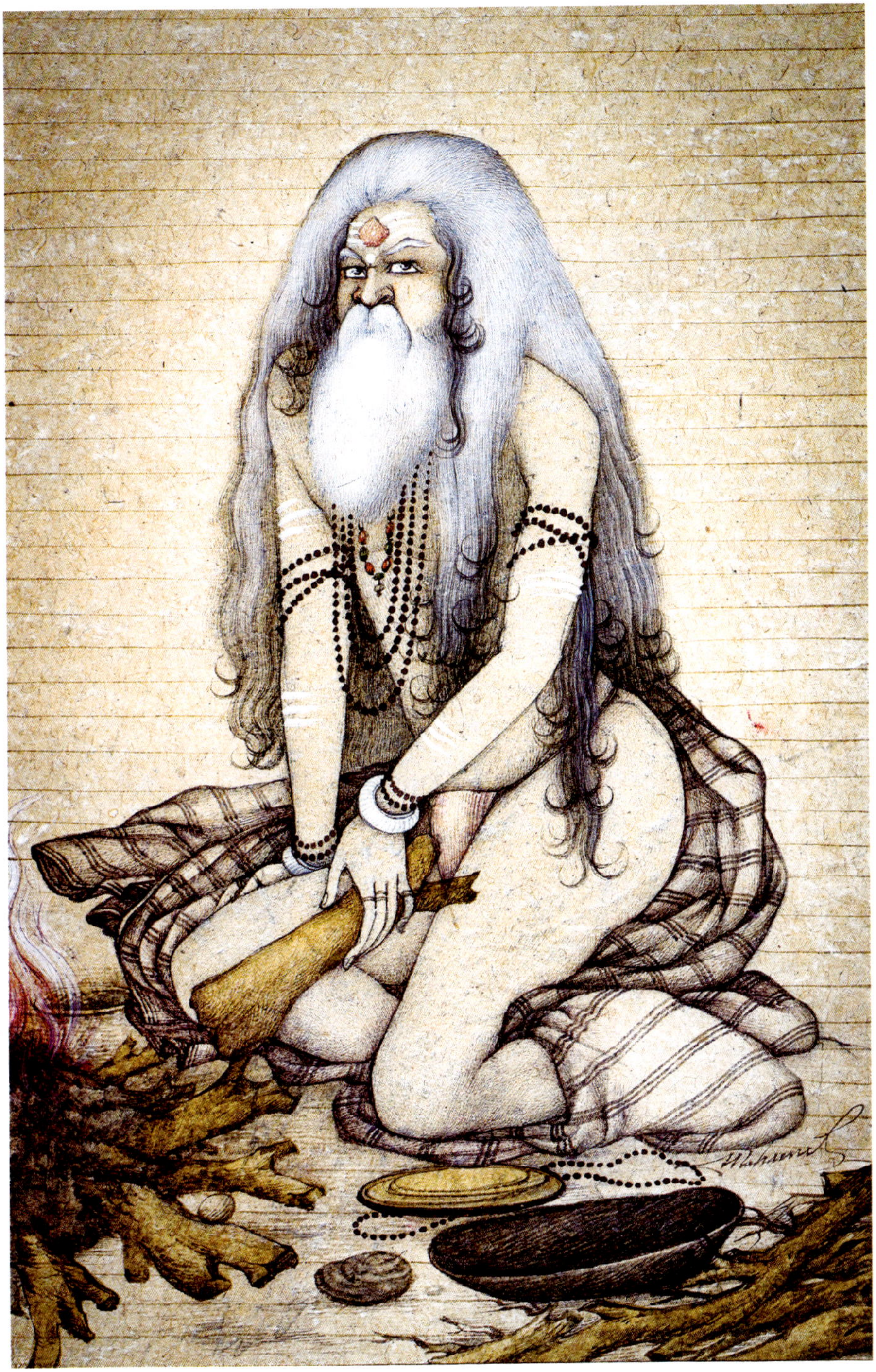

< Sadhu at the fire (I)
Natural pigments on handmade paper, 10x13cm

∧ Sadhu at the fire (II)
Natural pigments on handmade paper, 23x17cm

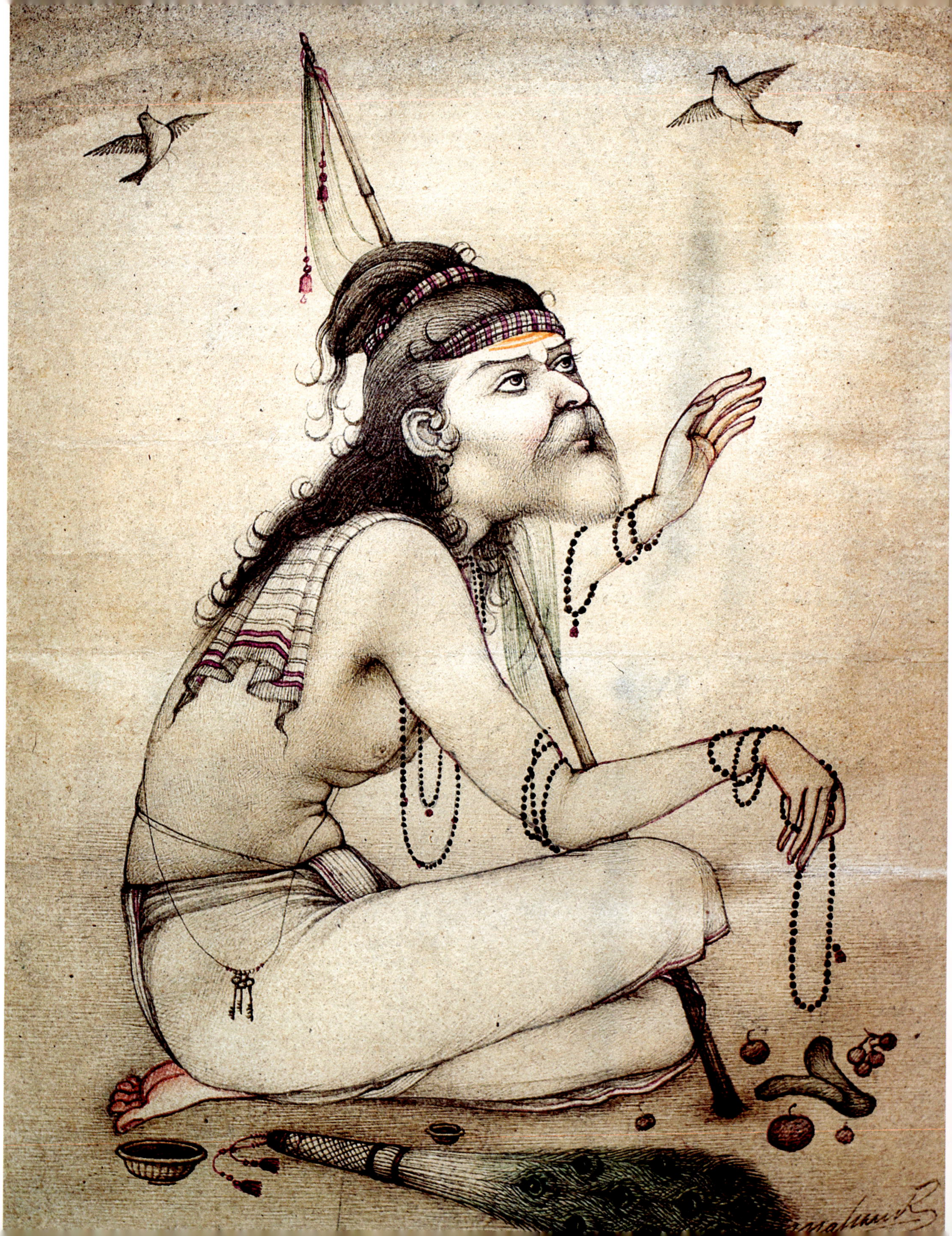

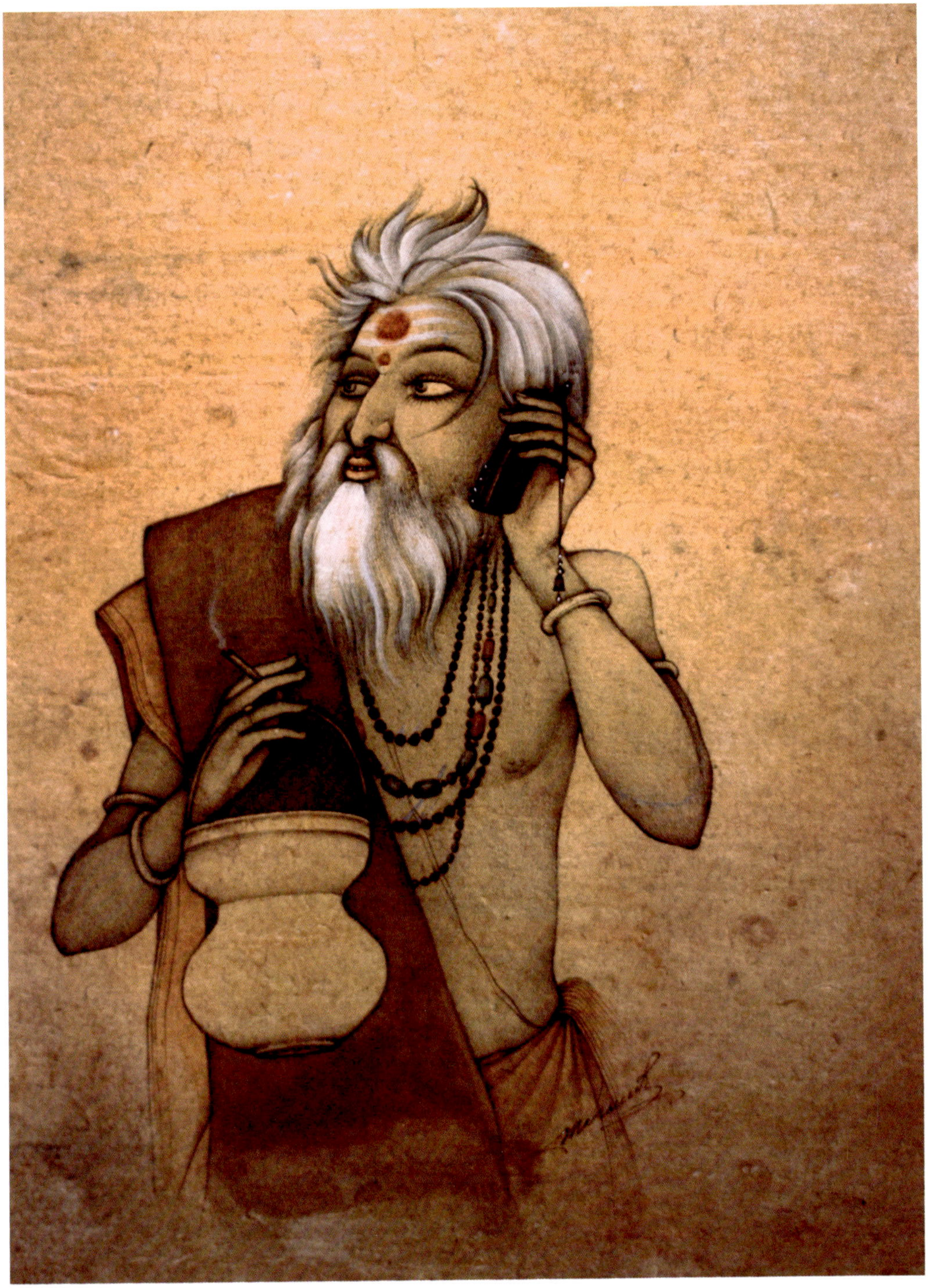

< Sadhu chanting on beads
Natural pigments on handmade paper, 16x13cm

∧ Sadhu on cellphone
Natural pigments on handmade paper, 16x13cm

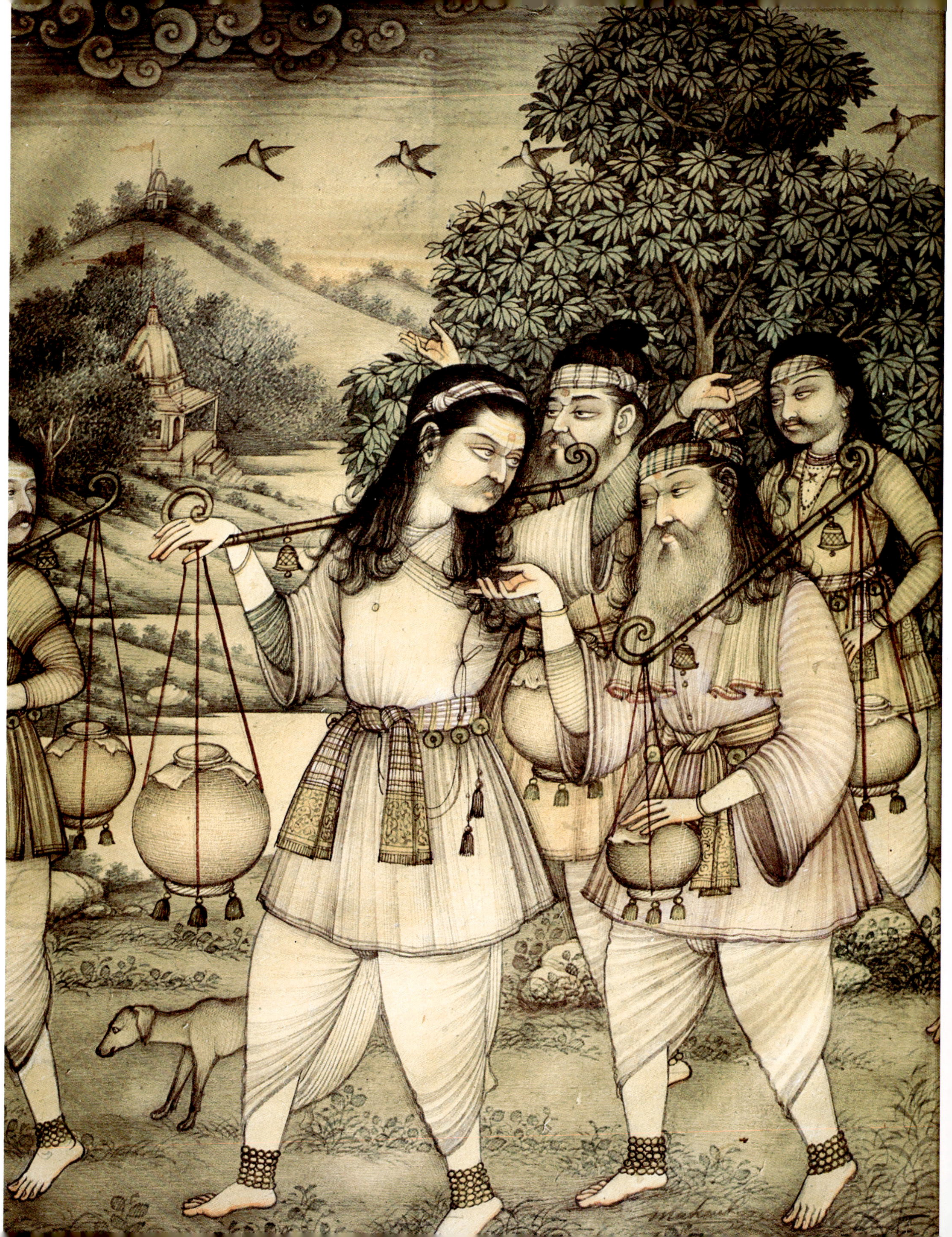

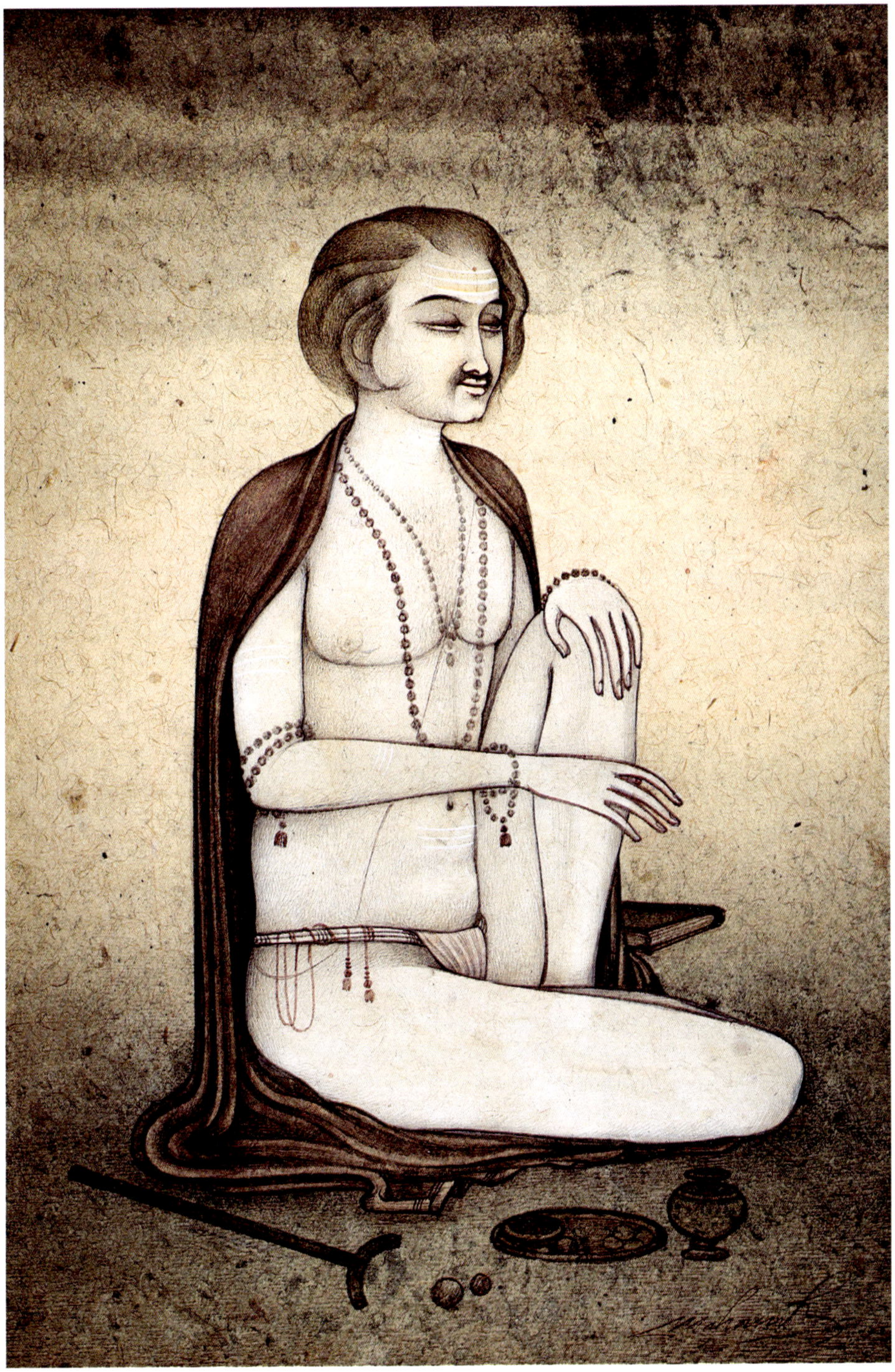

< Sadhus carrying pots
Natural pigments on handmade paper, 20x16cm

∧ Sadhu with chadar
Natural pigments on handmade paper, 16x11cm

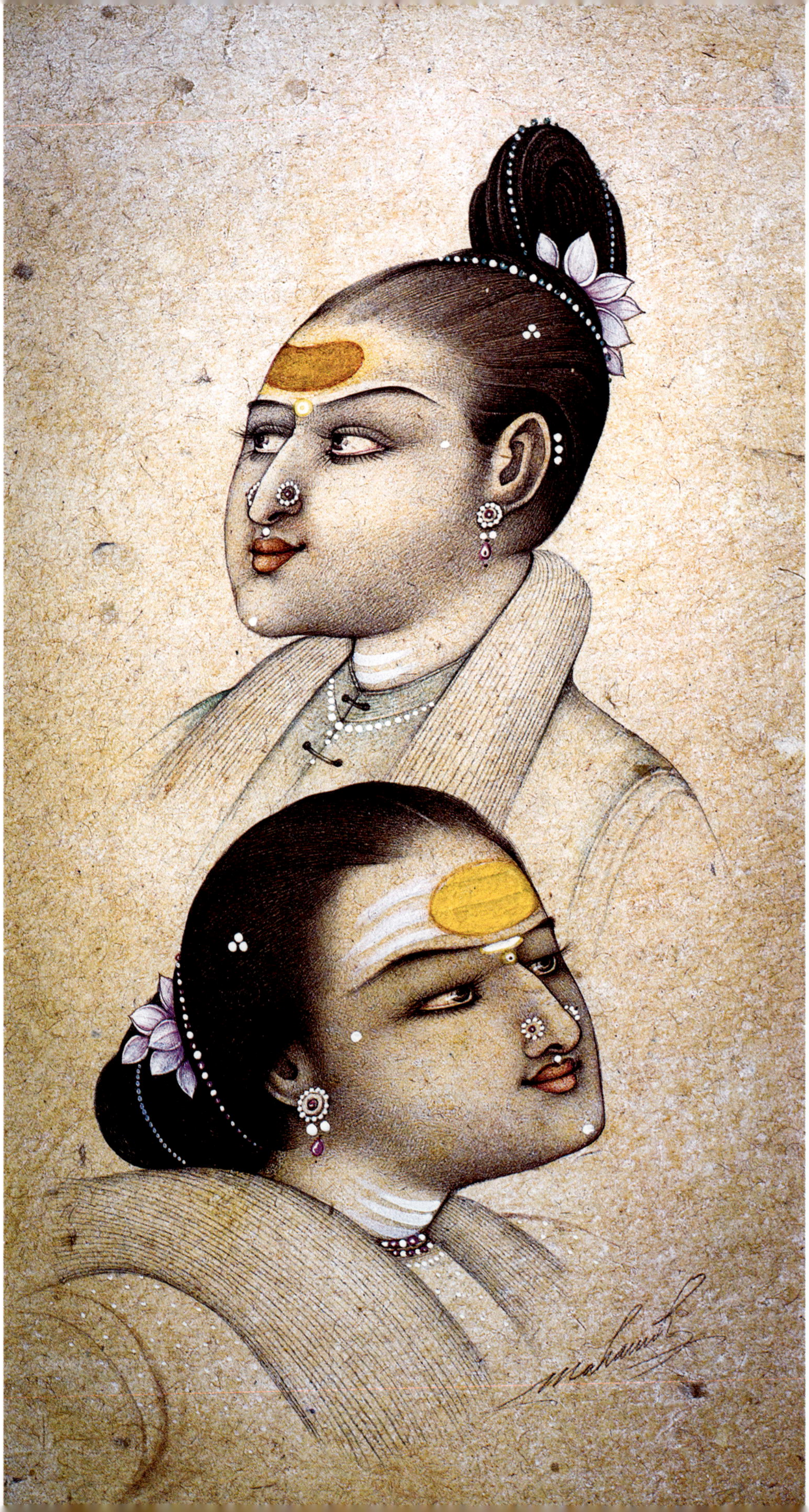

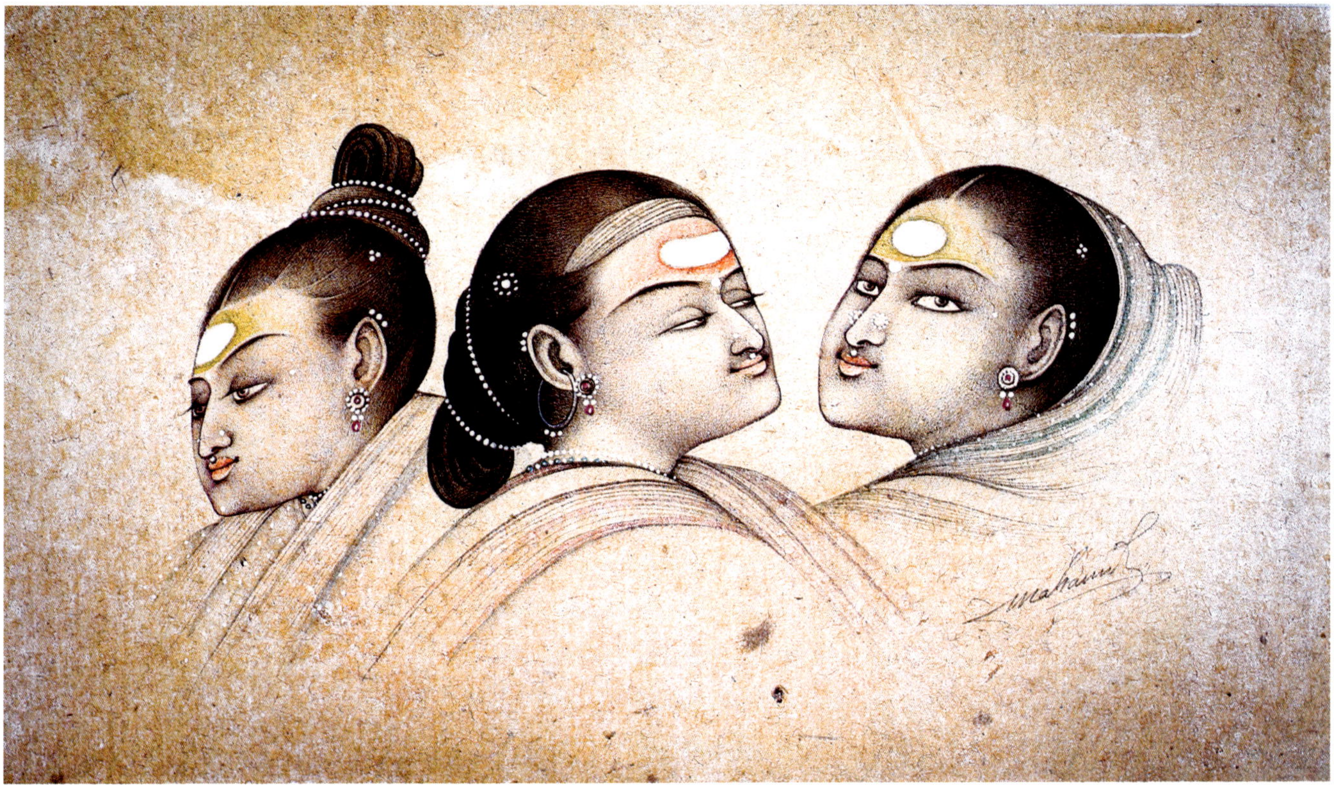

< Yoginis
Natural pigments on handmade paper, 23x13cm

∧ Yoginis
Natural pigments on handmade paper, 22x13cm

Kumba mela >
Natural pigments on vasli, 22x13cm

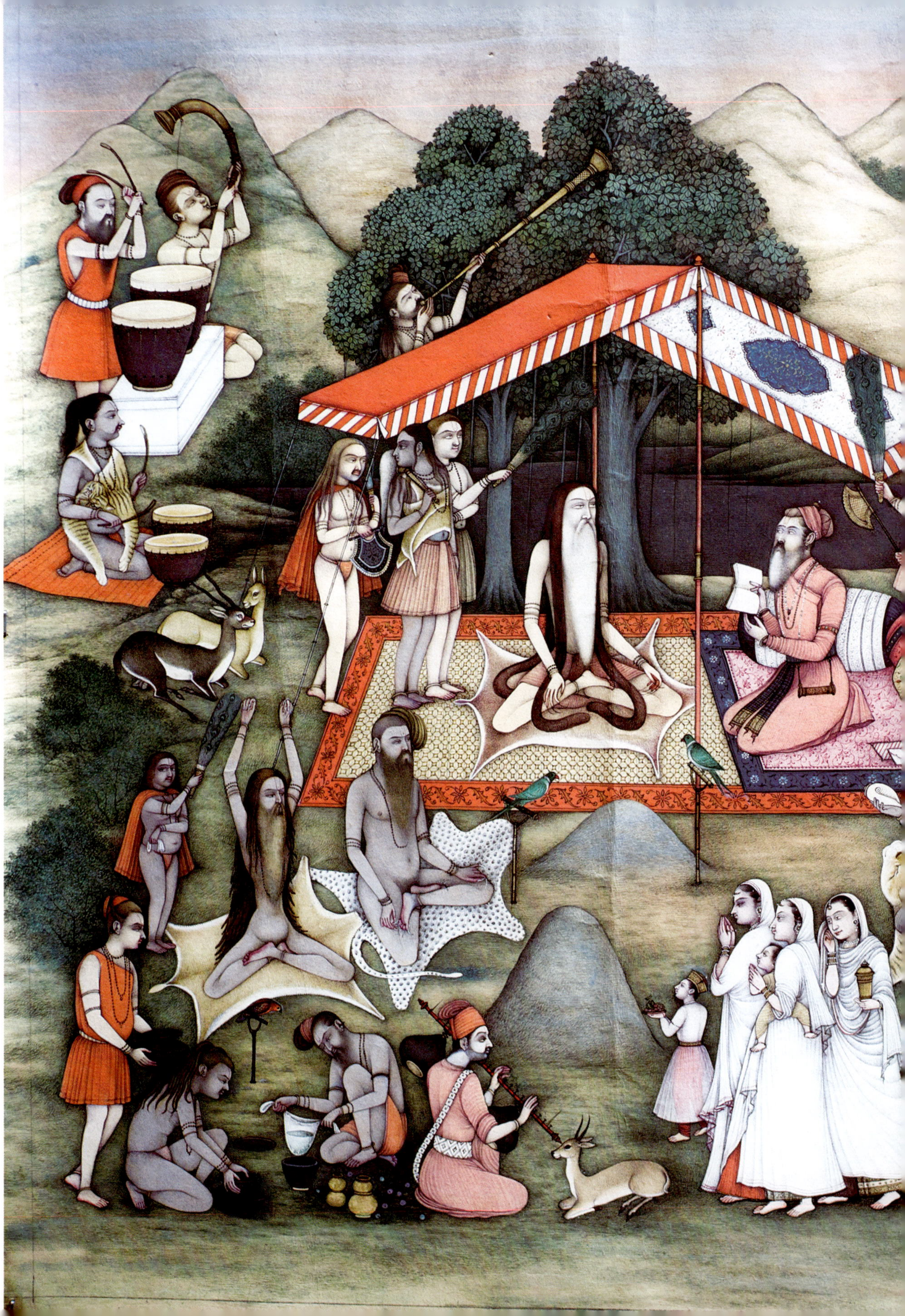

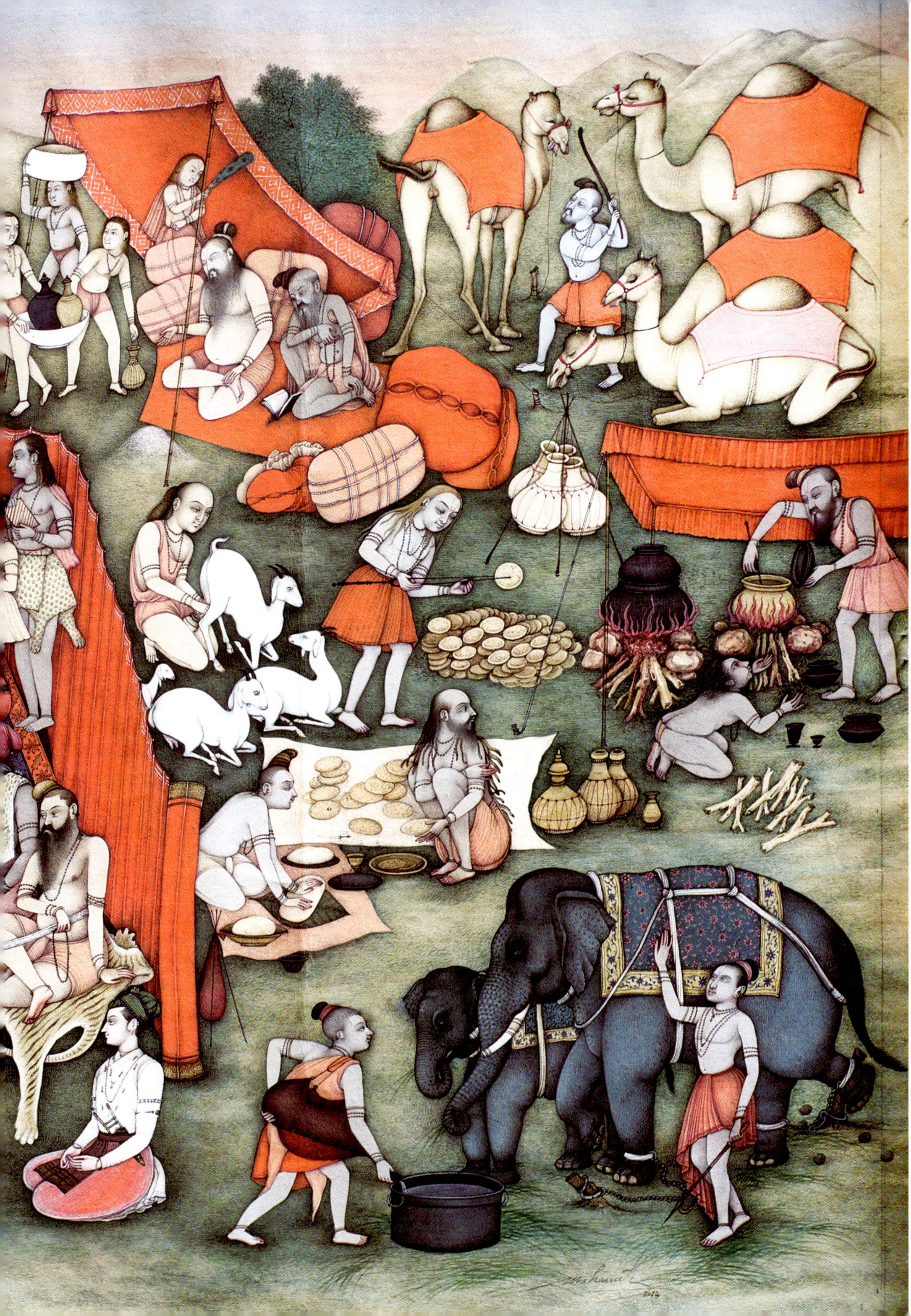

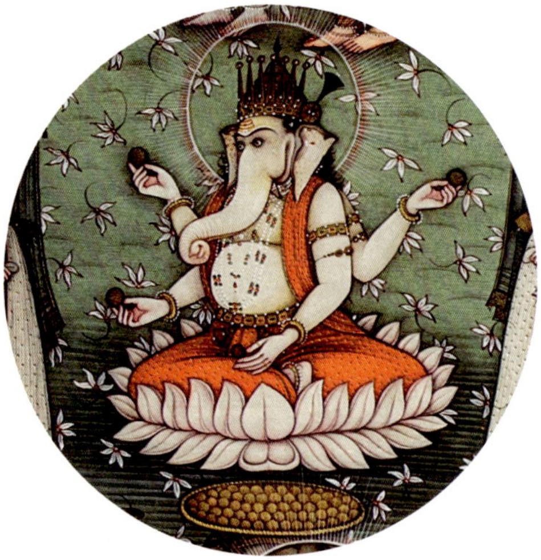

Mahayagna >
Pigments on handmade paper, 122x91cm

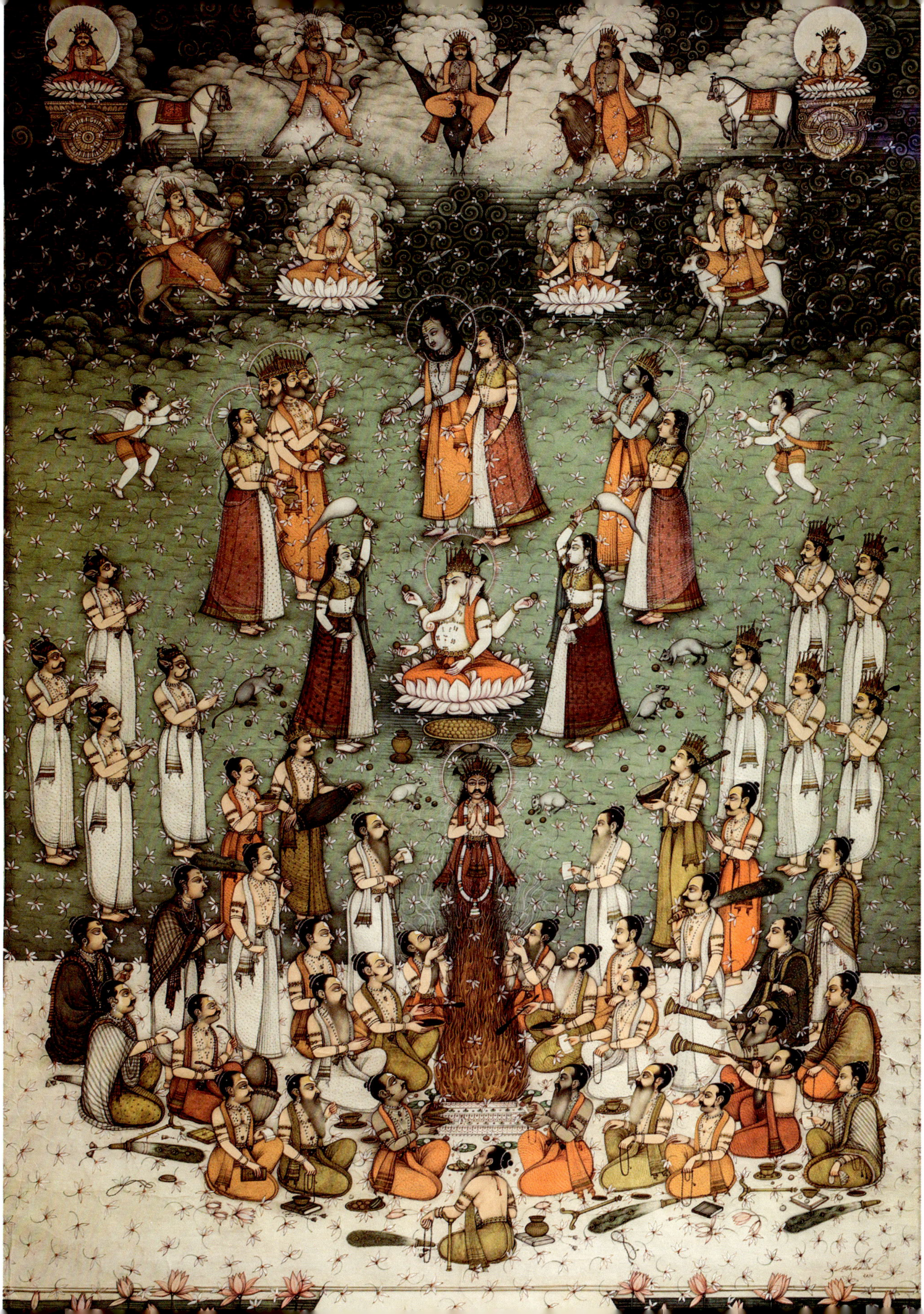

AVATARS

Four Kumaras >
Natural pigments on handmade paper, 23x13cm

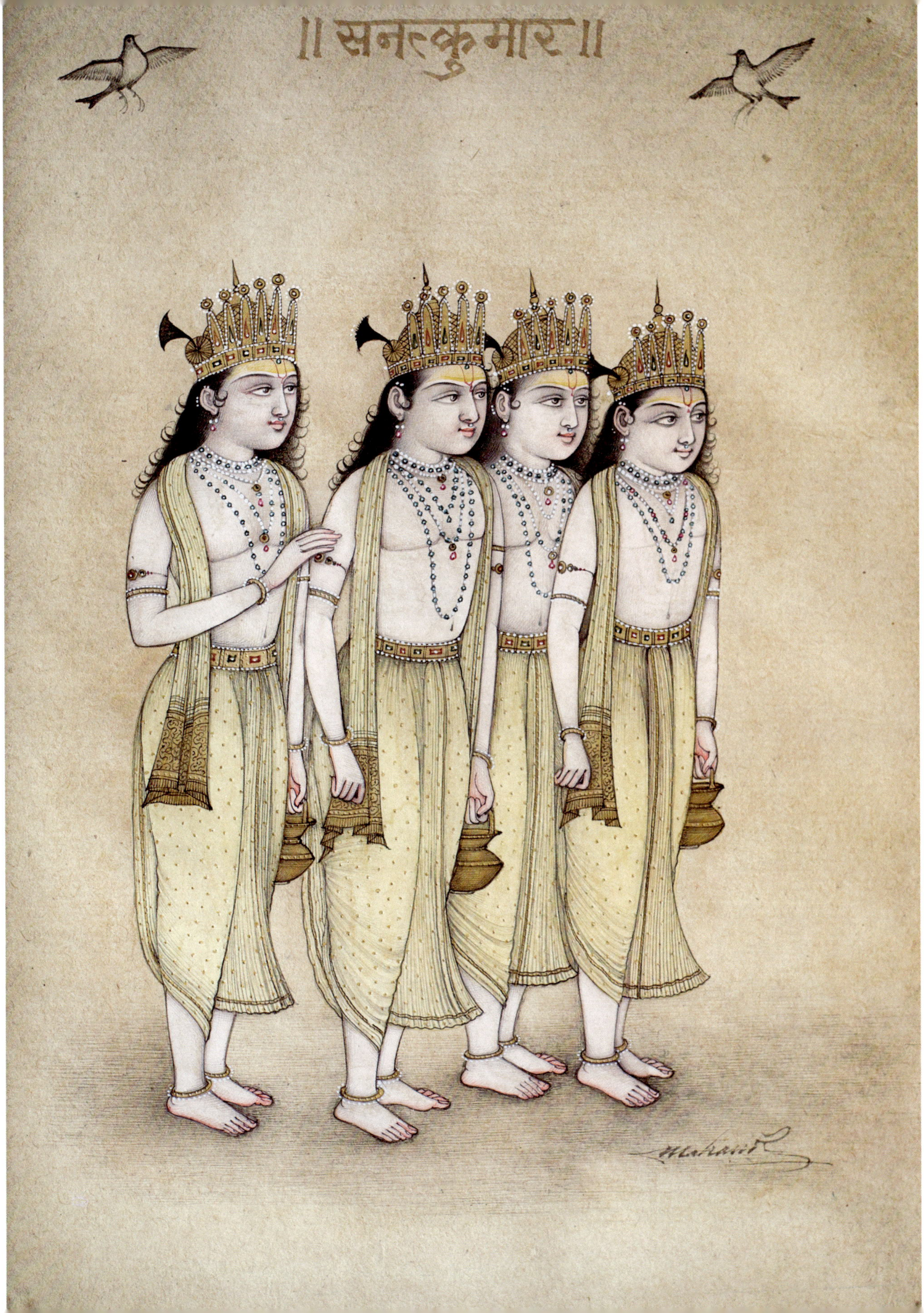
॥ सनत्कुमार ॥

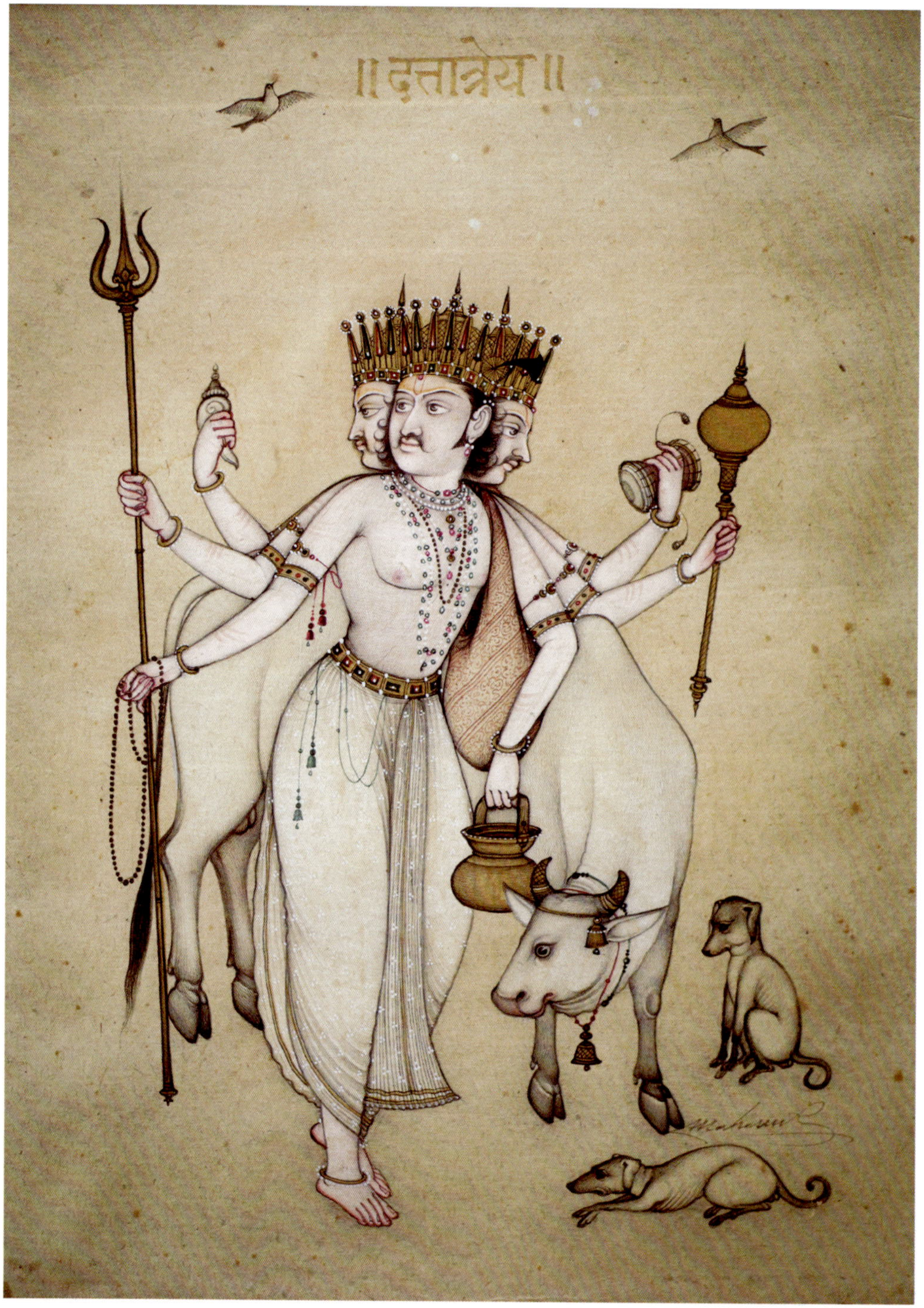

Dattatreya
Natural pigments on handmade paper, 23x13cm

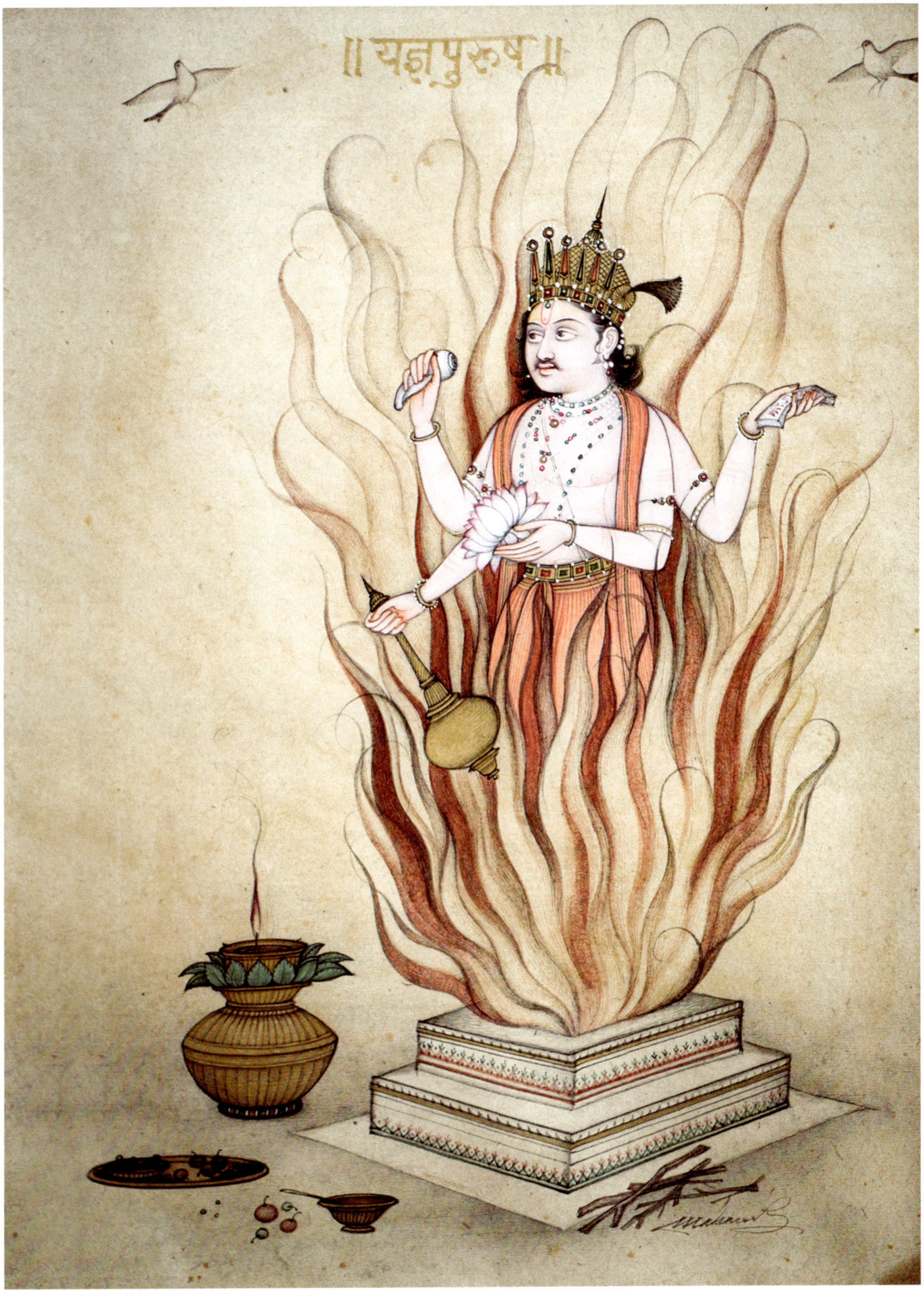

Yajna
Natural pigments on handmade paper, 23x13cm

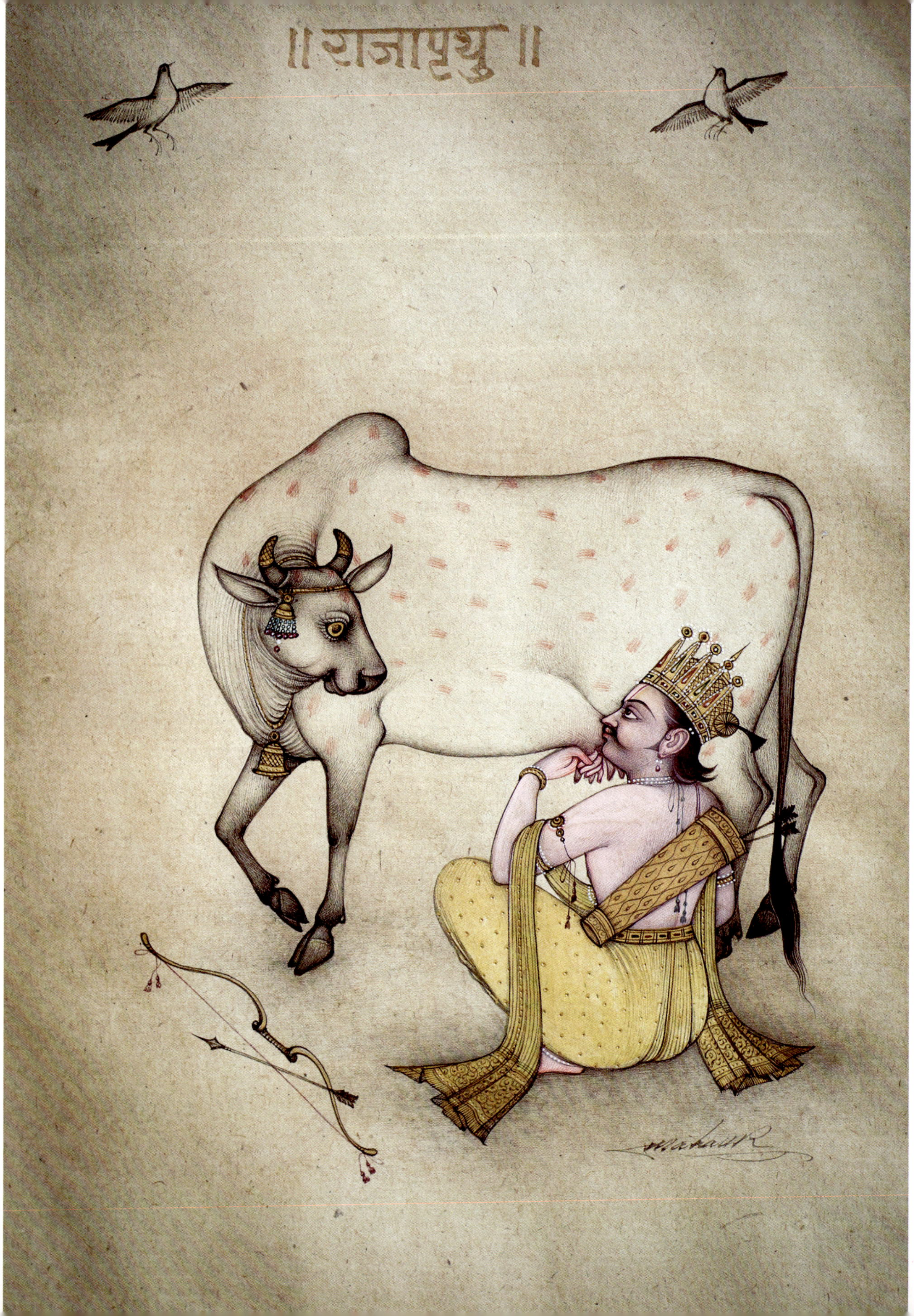
॥ राजापृथु ॥

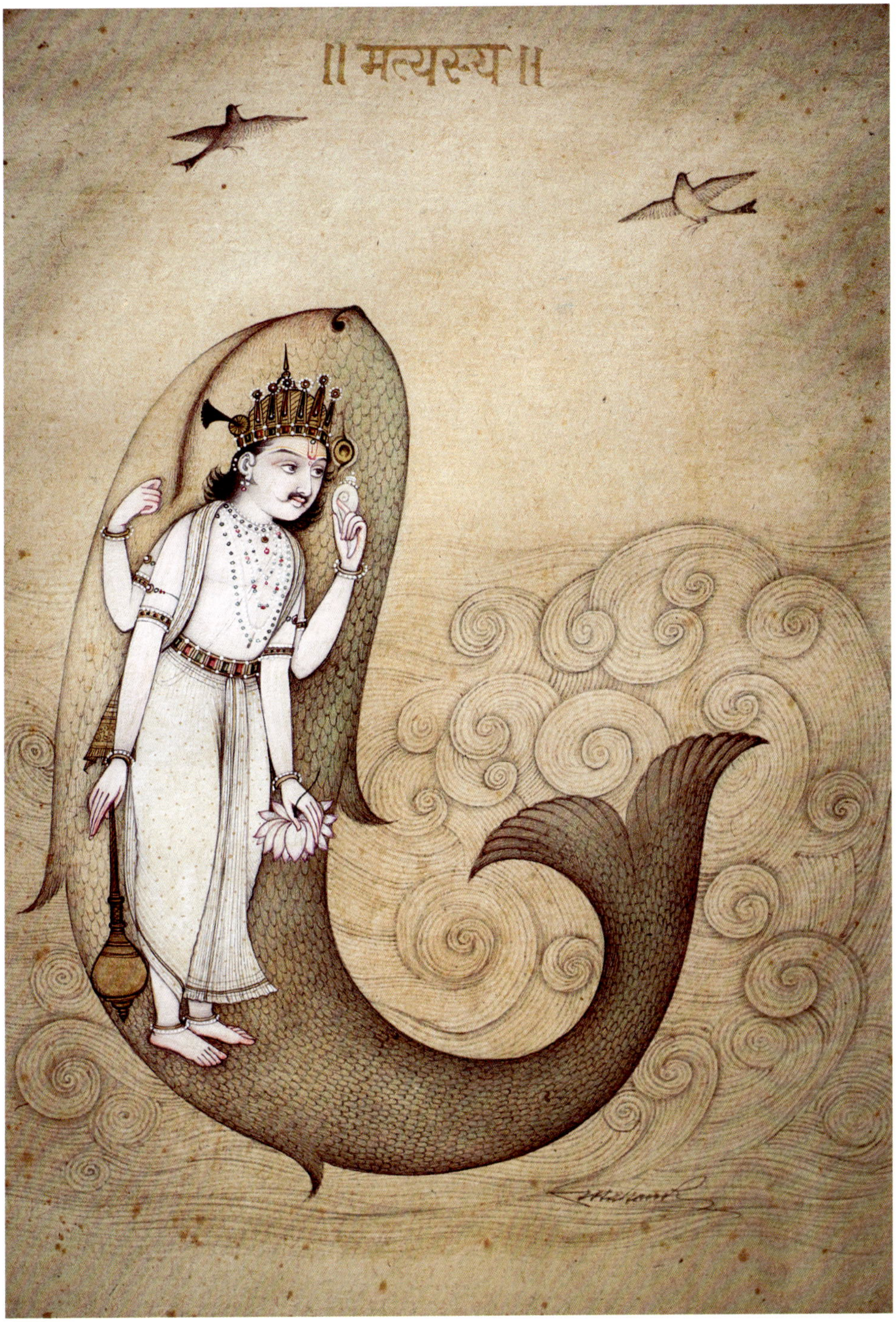

< Prthu
Natural pigments on handmade paper, 23x13cm

∧ Matsya
Natural pigments on handmade paper, 22x13cm

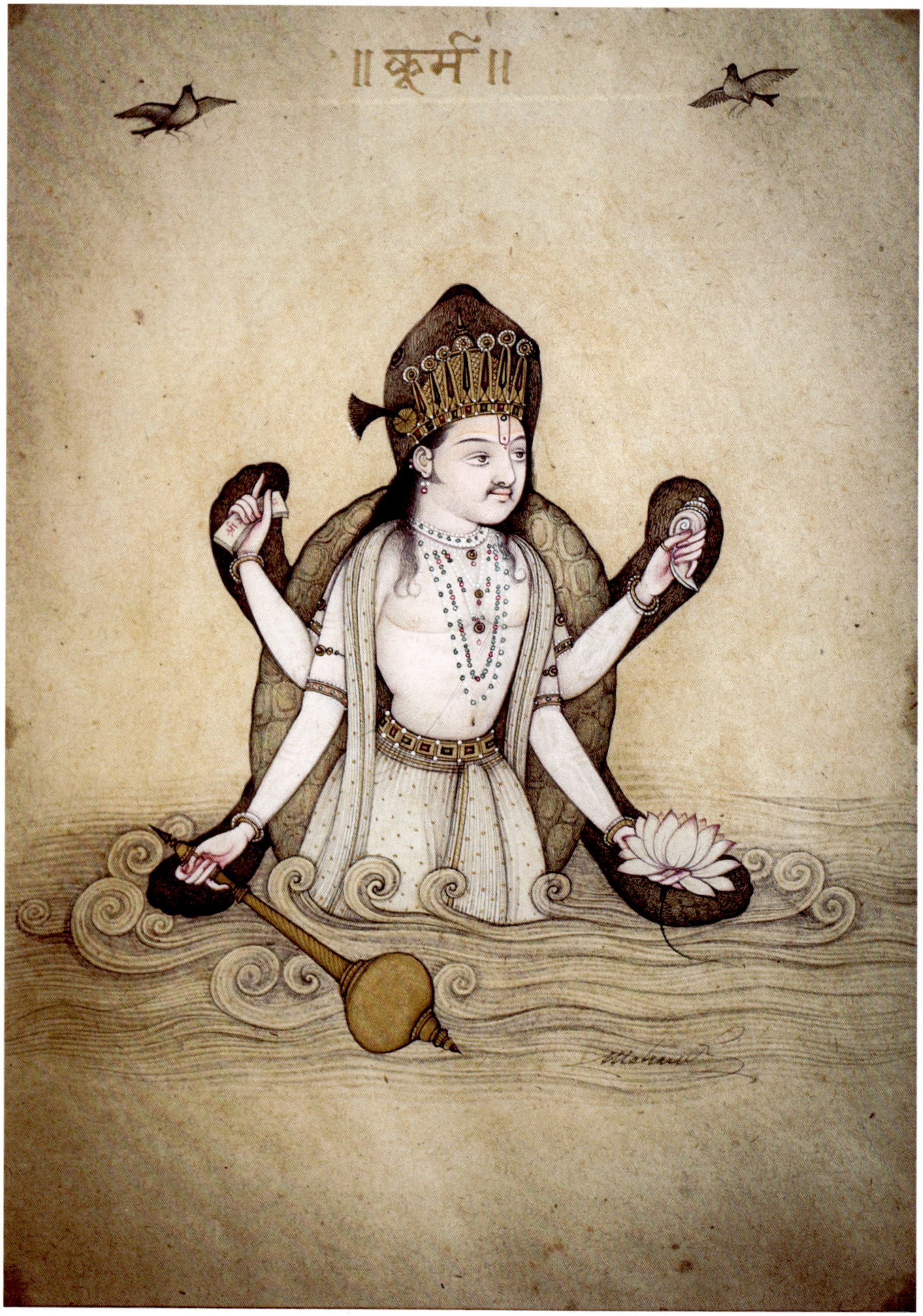

Kurma
Natural pigments on handmade paper, 23x13cm

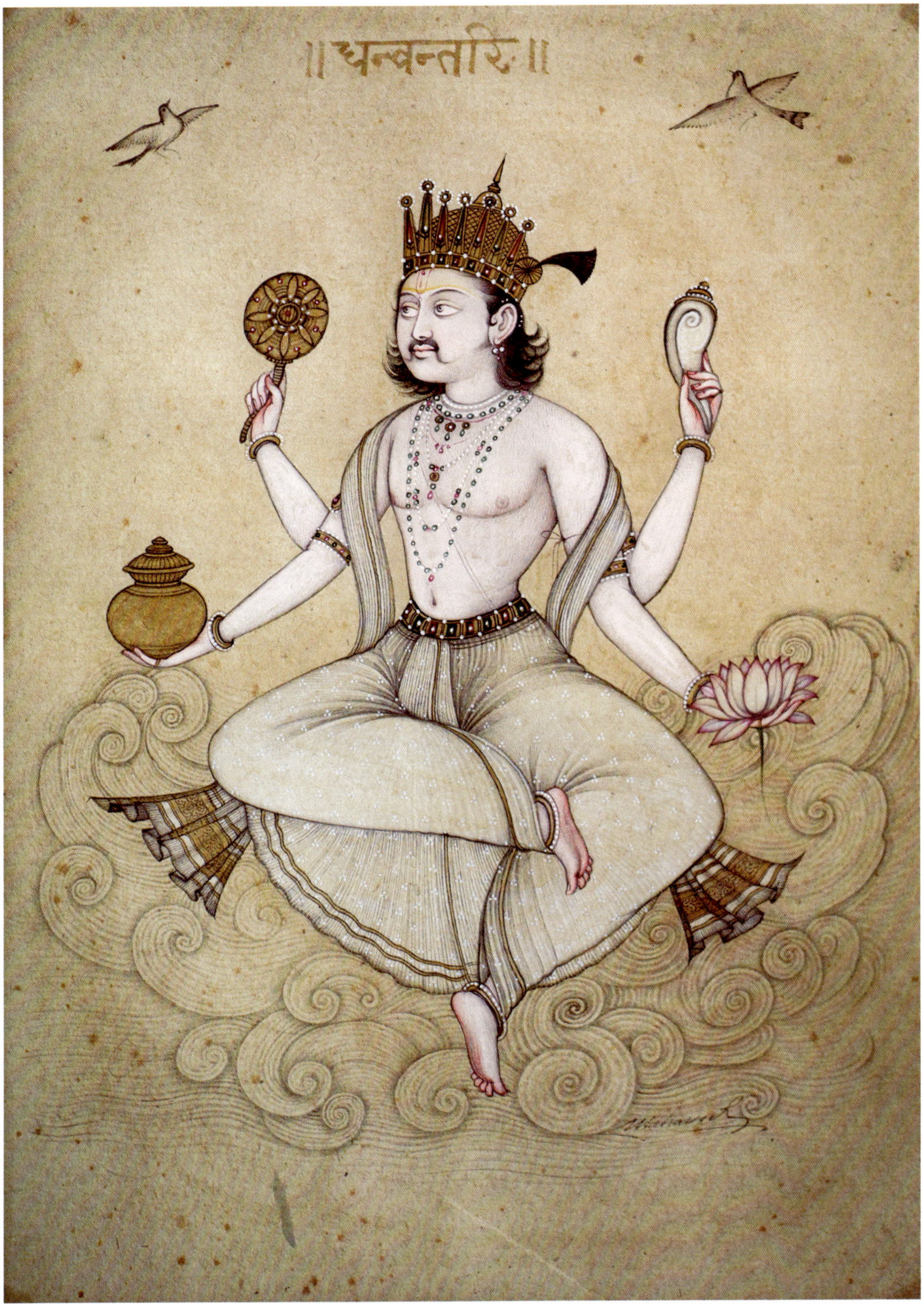

Dhanvantari
Natural pigments on handmade paper, 23x13cm

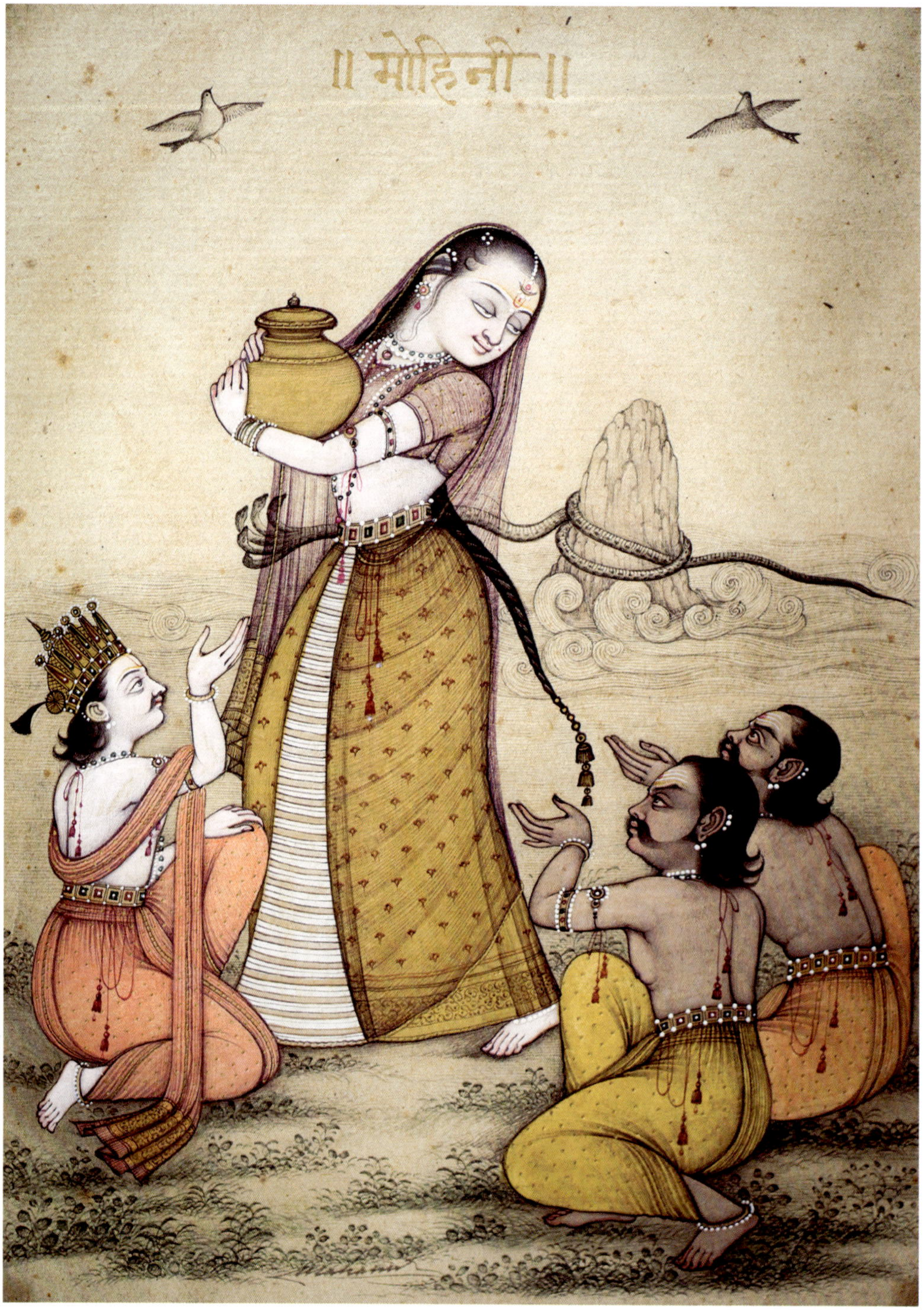

∧ Mohini
Natural pigments on handmade paper, 23x13cm

Nrsimha >
Natural pigments on handmade paper, 23x13cm

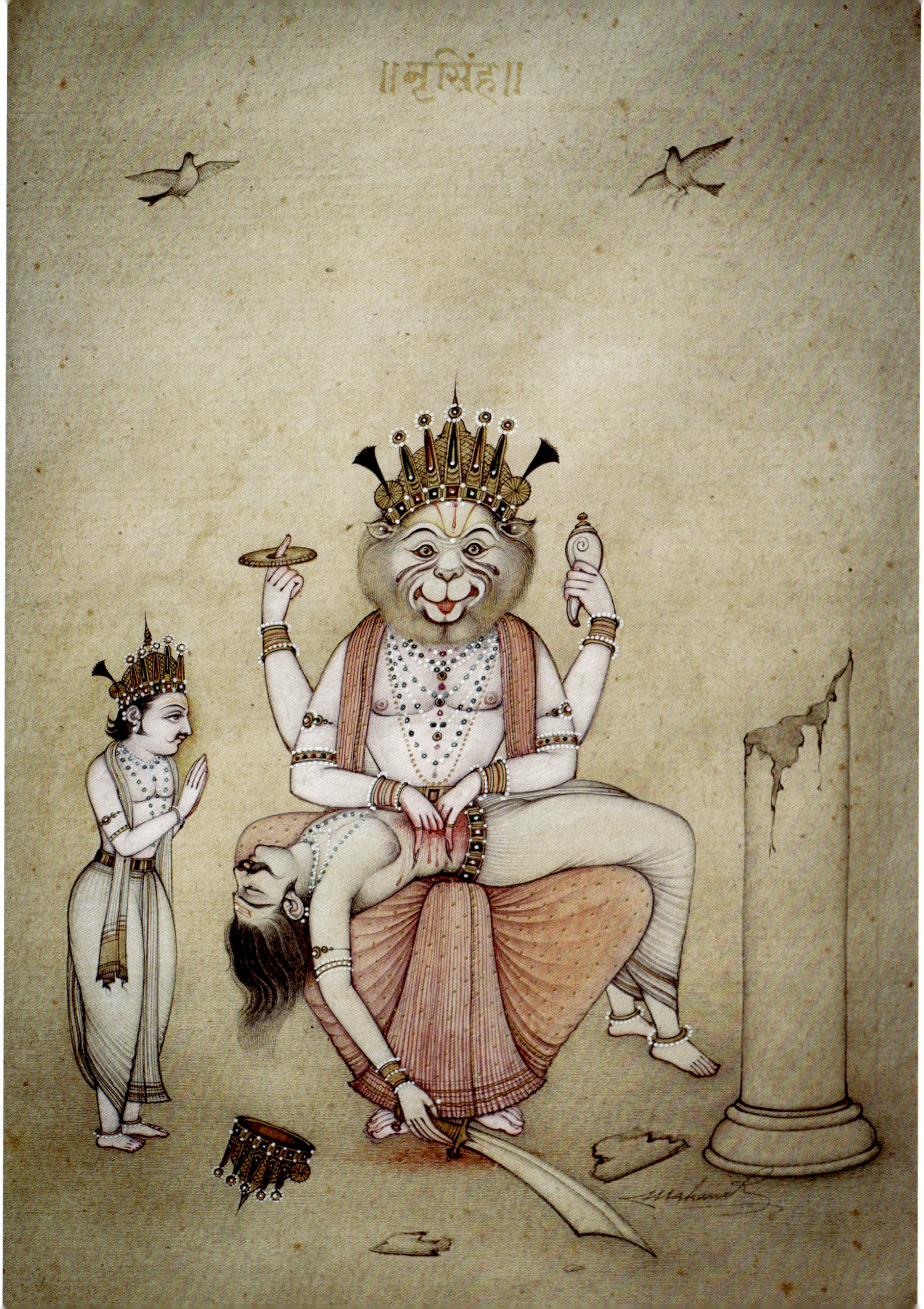
।।नृसिंह।।

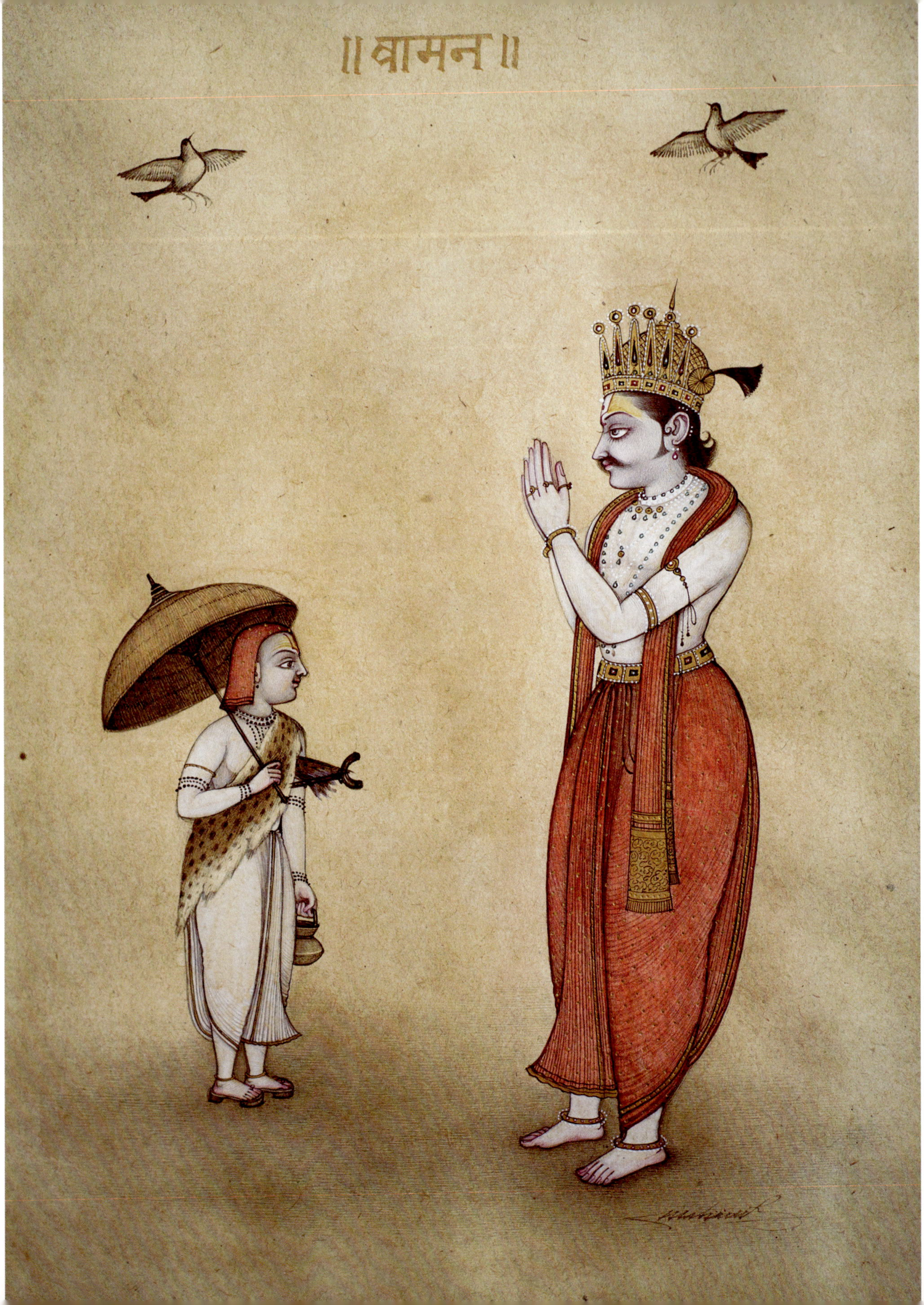
॥ वामन ॥

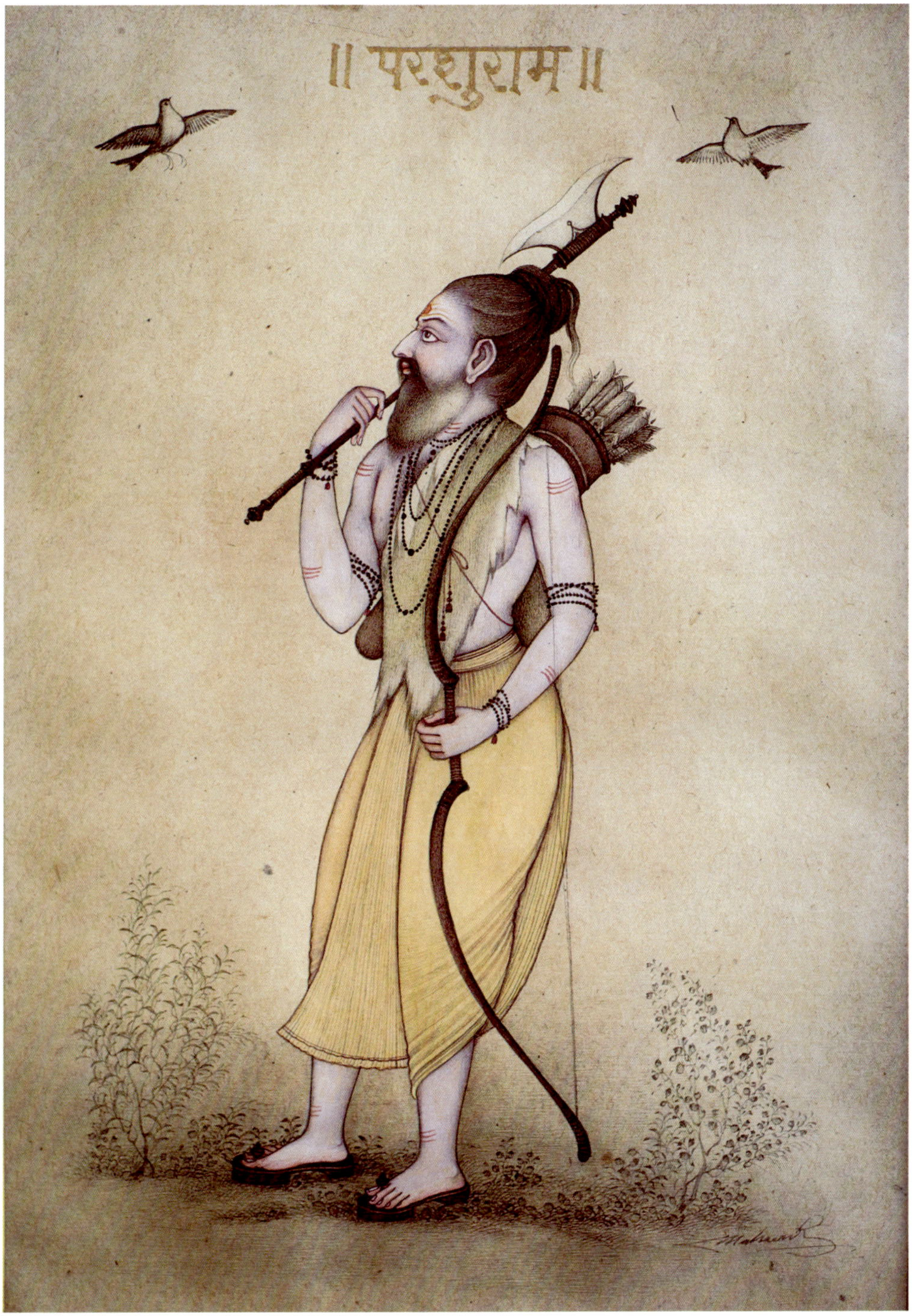

< Vamana
Natural pigments on handmade paper, 23x13cm

∧ Parasurama
Natural pigments on handmade paper, 23x13cm

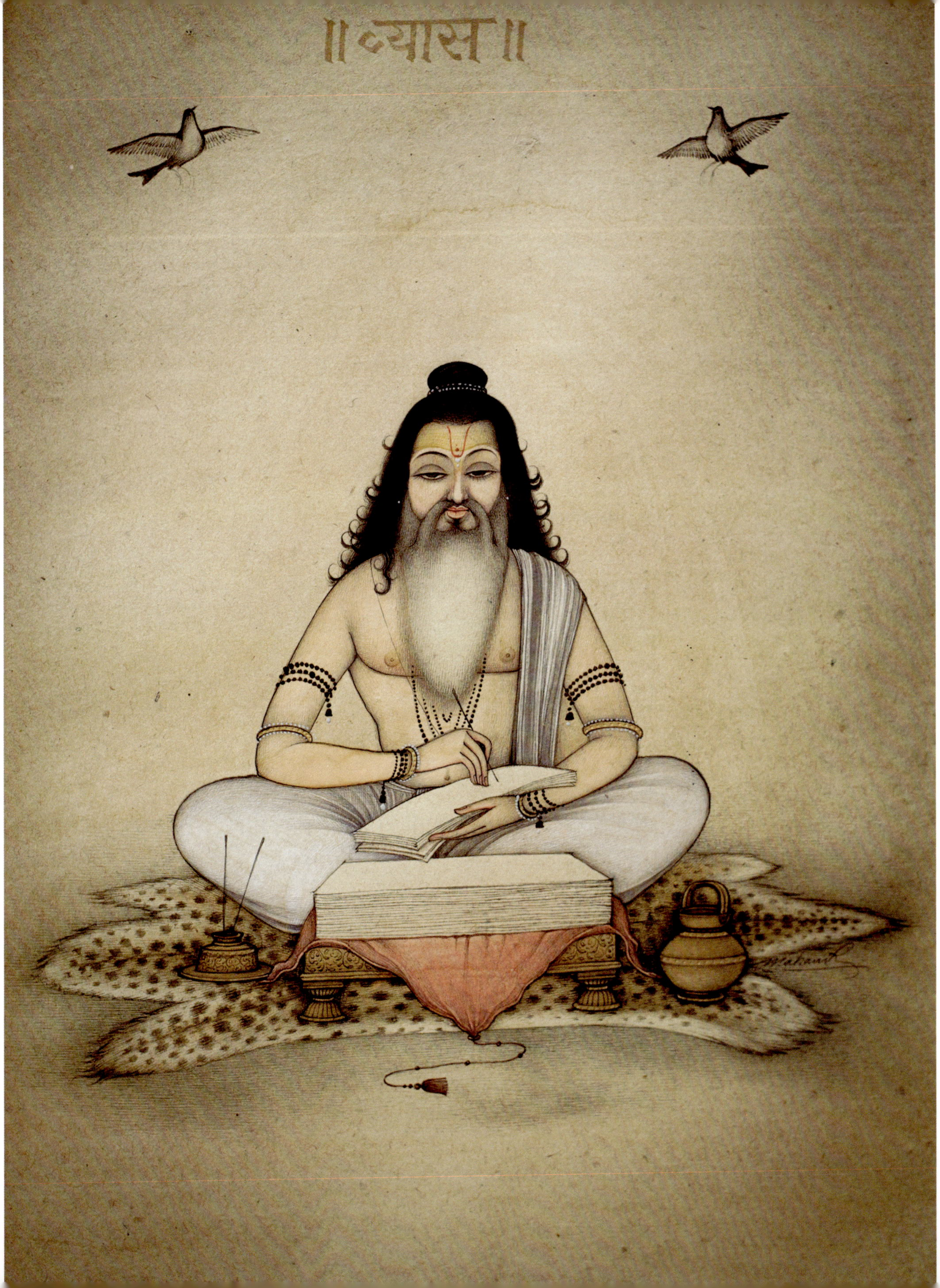
॥ व्यास ॥

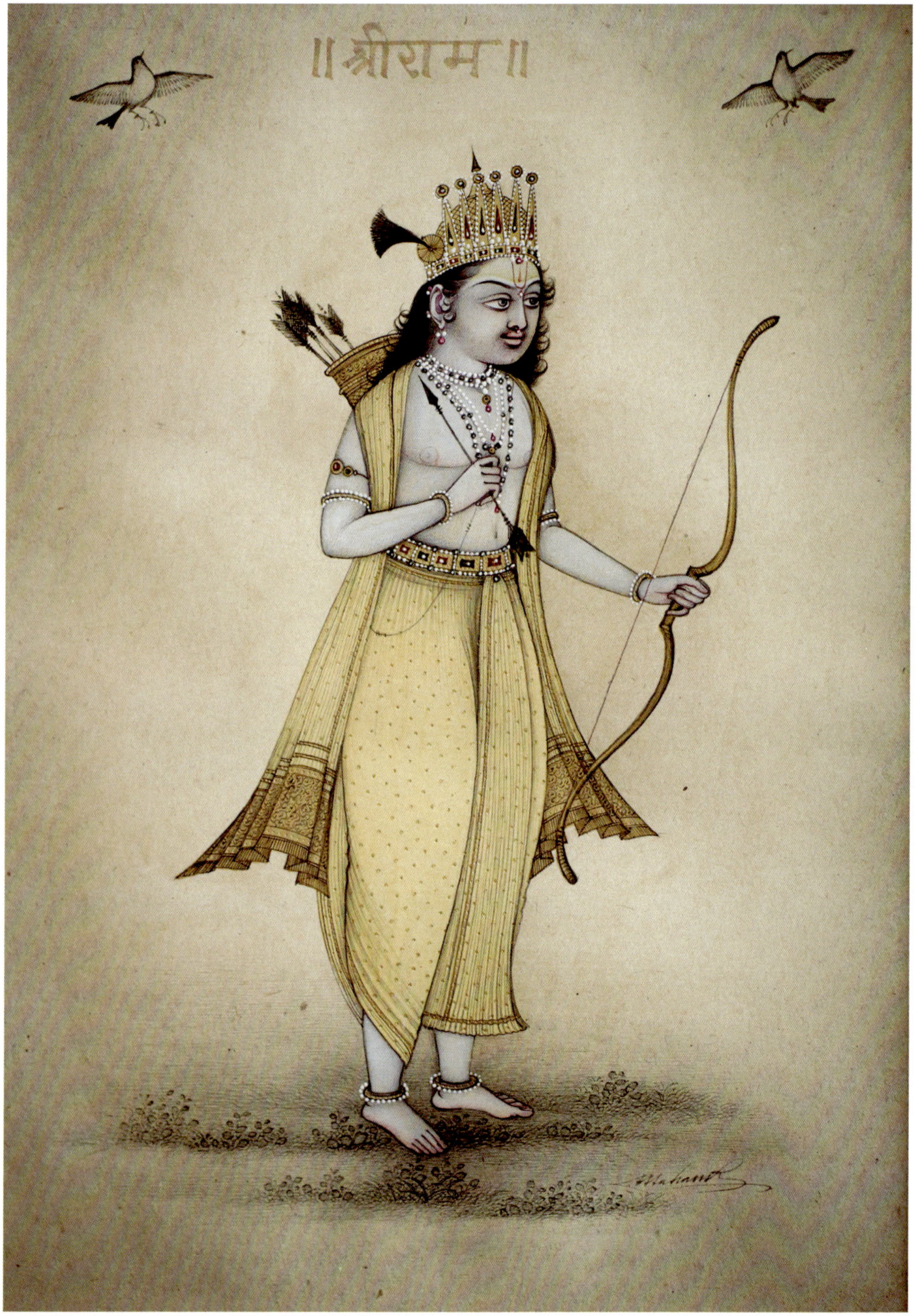

< Vyasadeva
Natural pigments on handmade paper, 23x13cm

∧ Rama
Natural pigments on handmade paper, 23x13cm

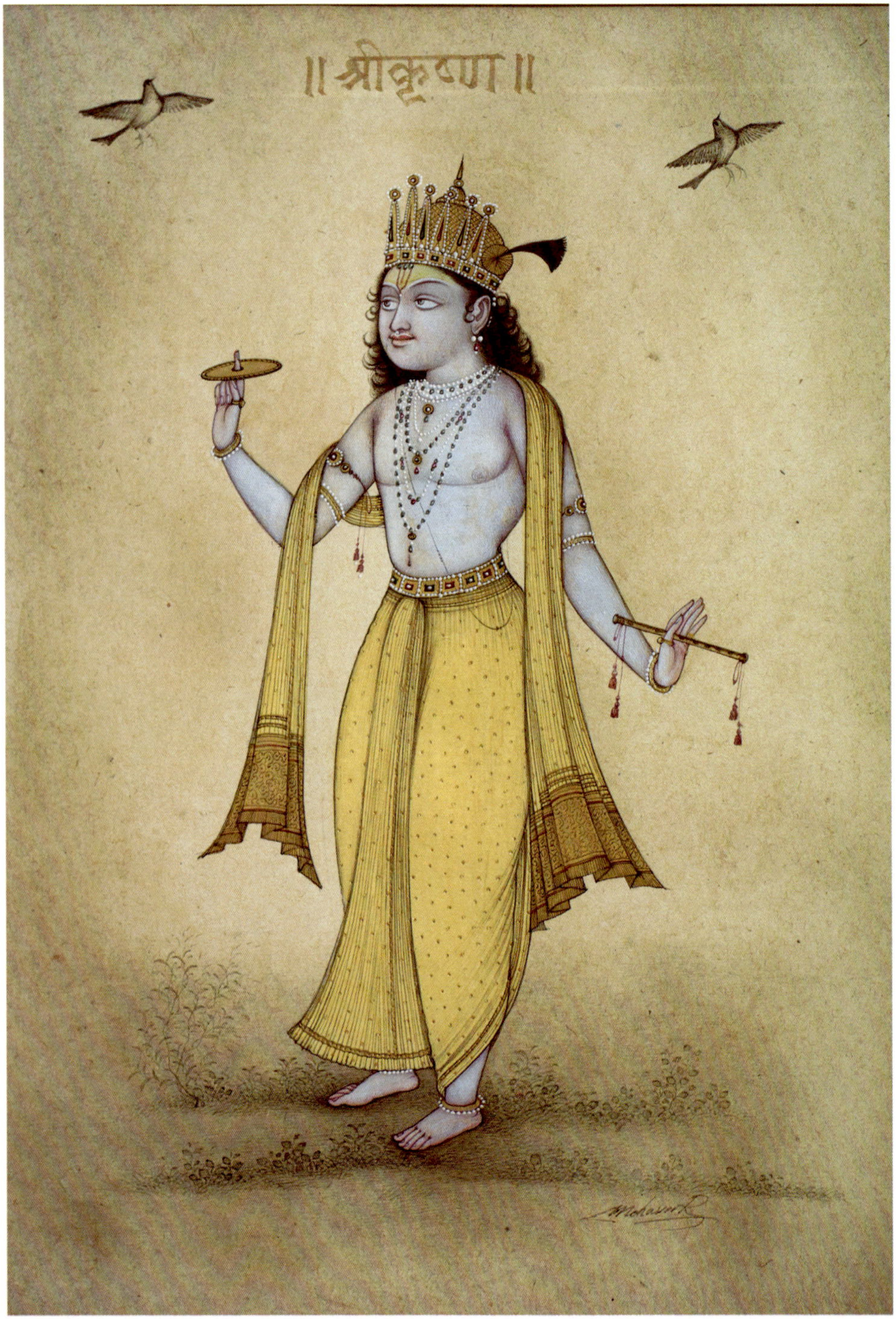

∧ Krsna
Natural pigments on handmade paper, 23x13cm

Buddha >
Natural pigments on handmade paper, 23x13cm

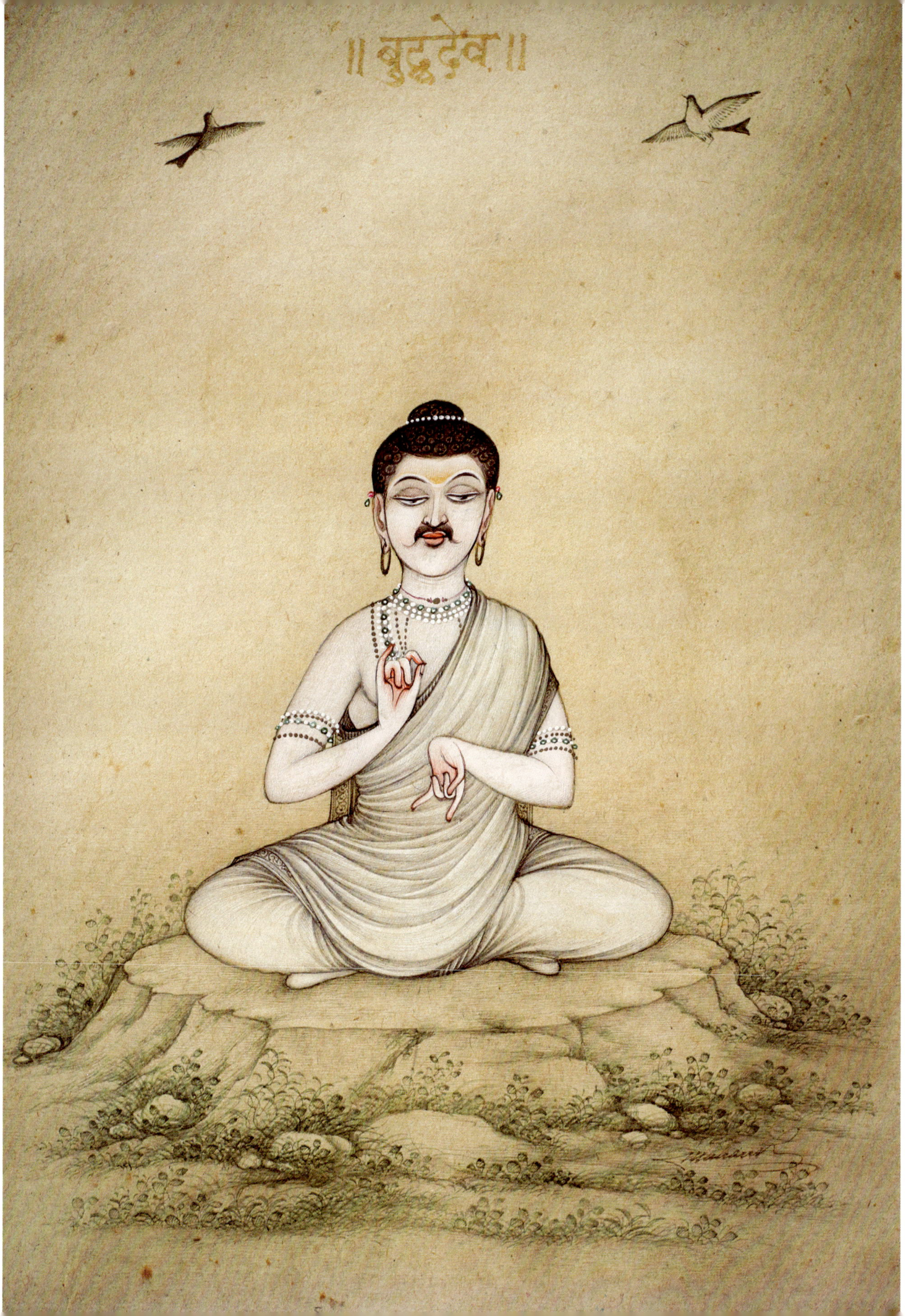
॥ बुद्धदेव ॥

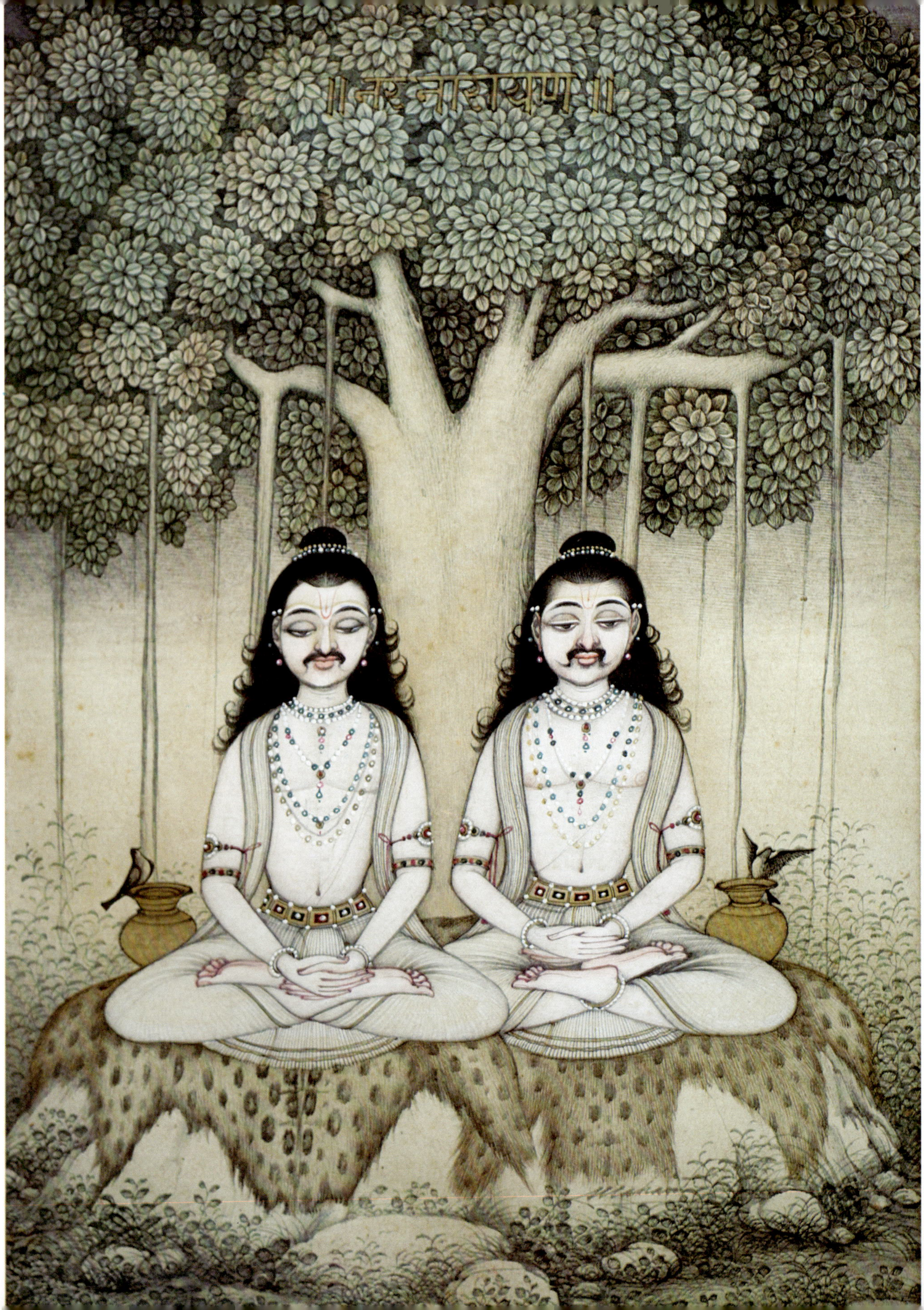
॥ नर नारायण ॥

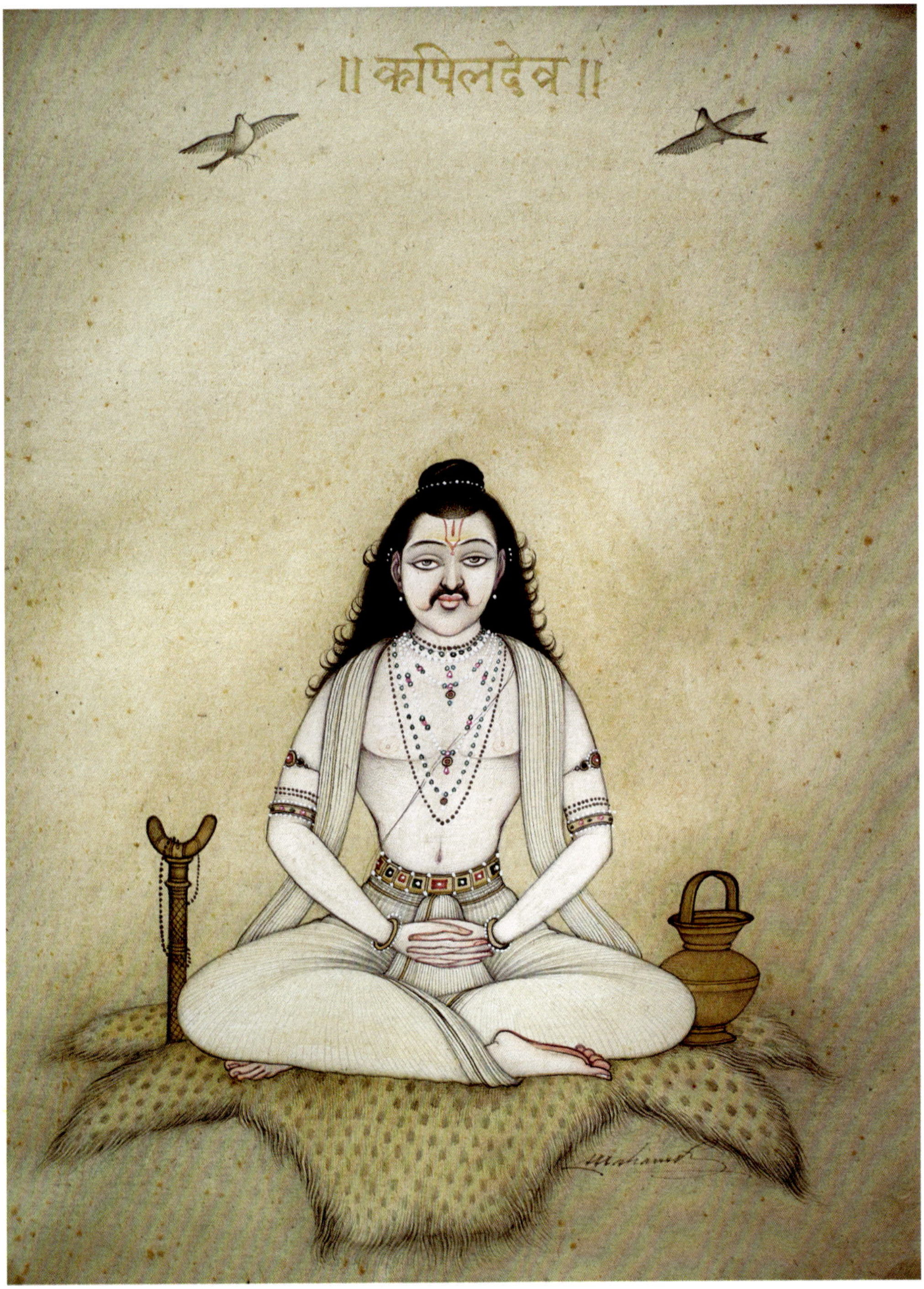

< Nara-Narayana
Natural pigments on handmade paper, 23x13cm

∧ Kapila
Natural pigments on handmade paper, 23x13cm

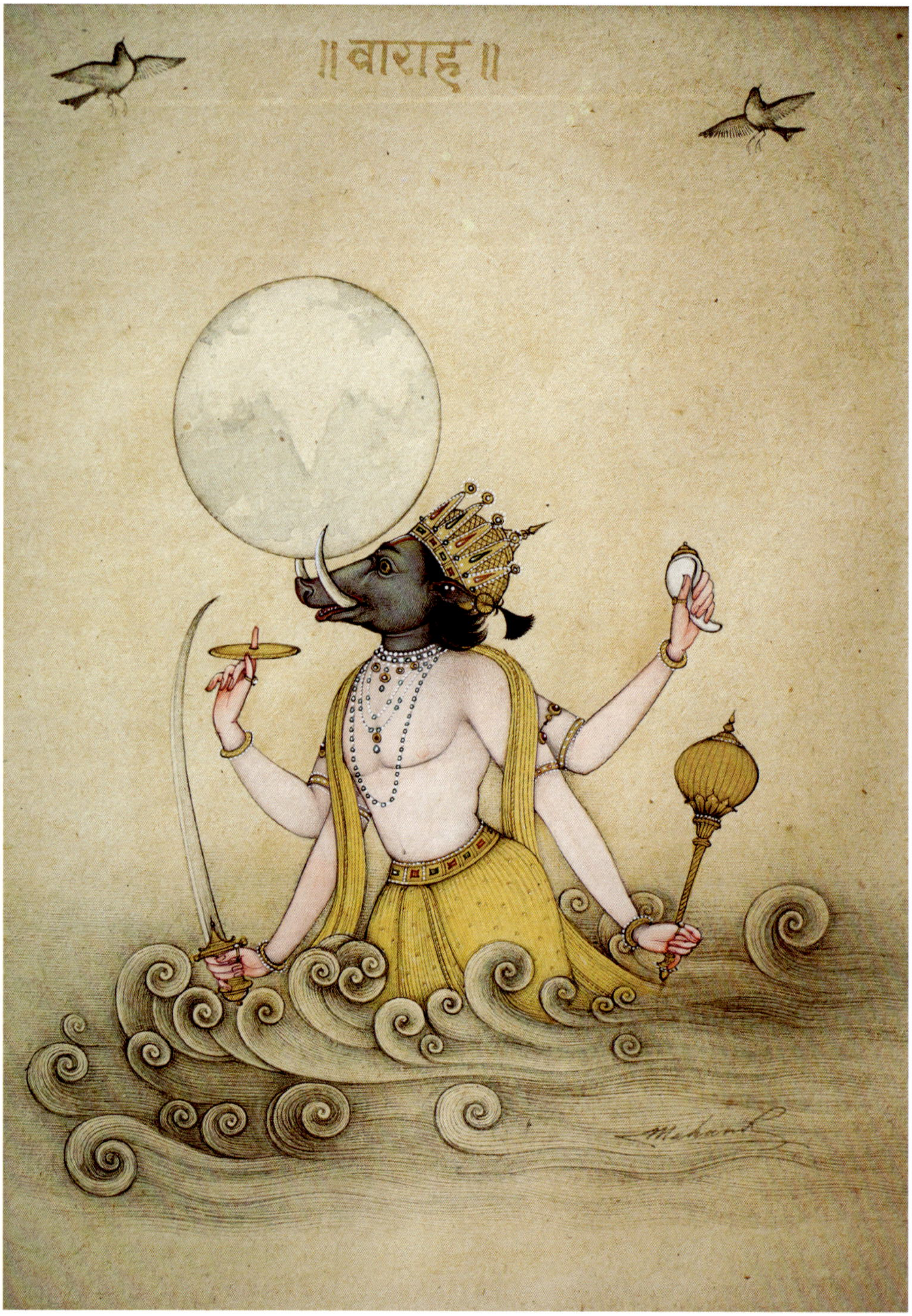

∧Varaha
Natural pigments on handmade paper, 22.5x13cm

Narada Muni >
Natural pigments on handmade paper, 23x13cm

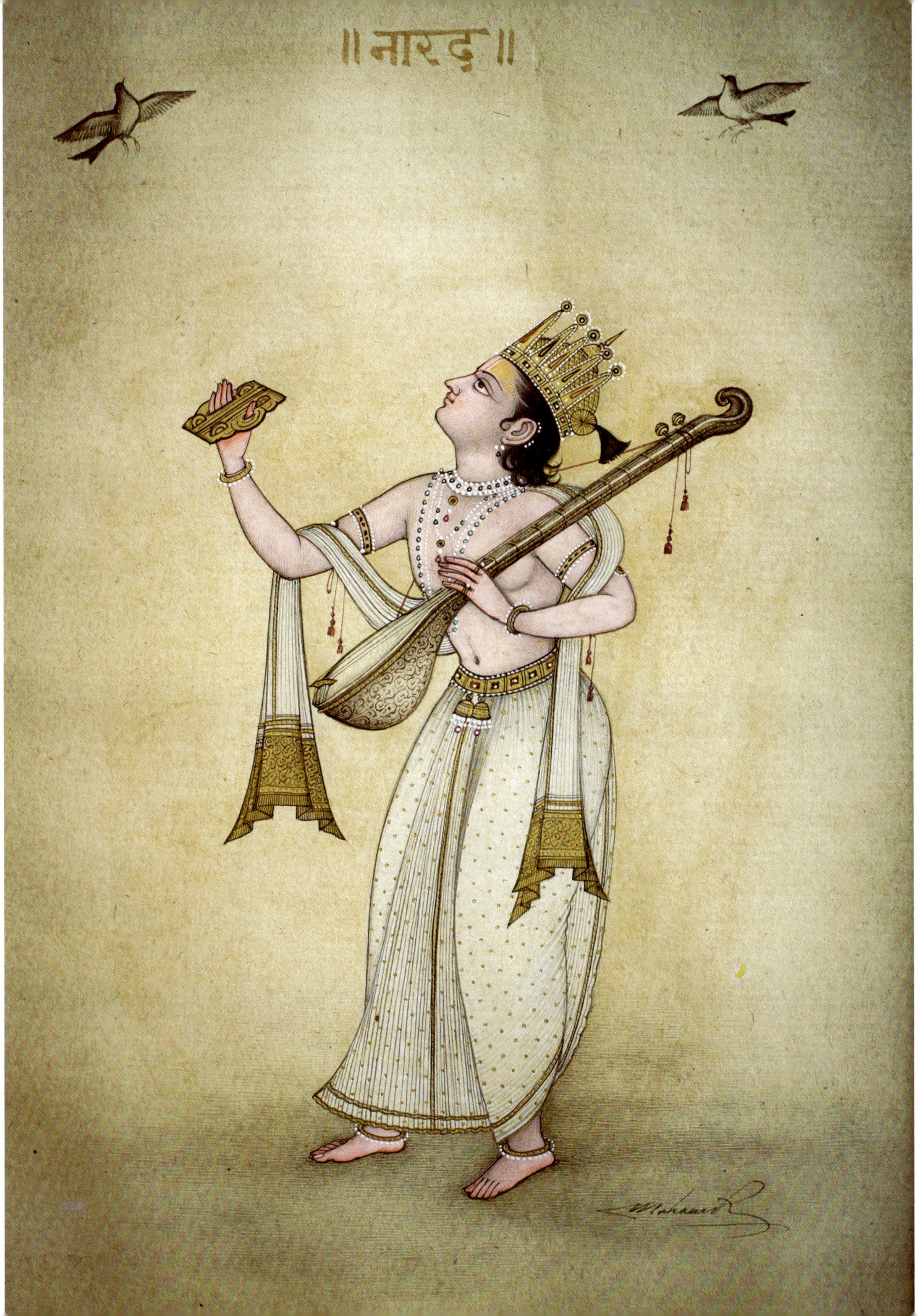
॥ नारद ॥

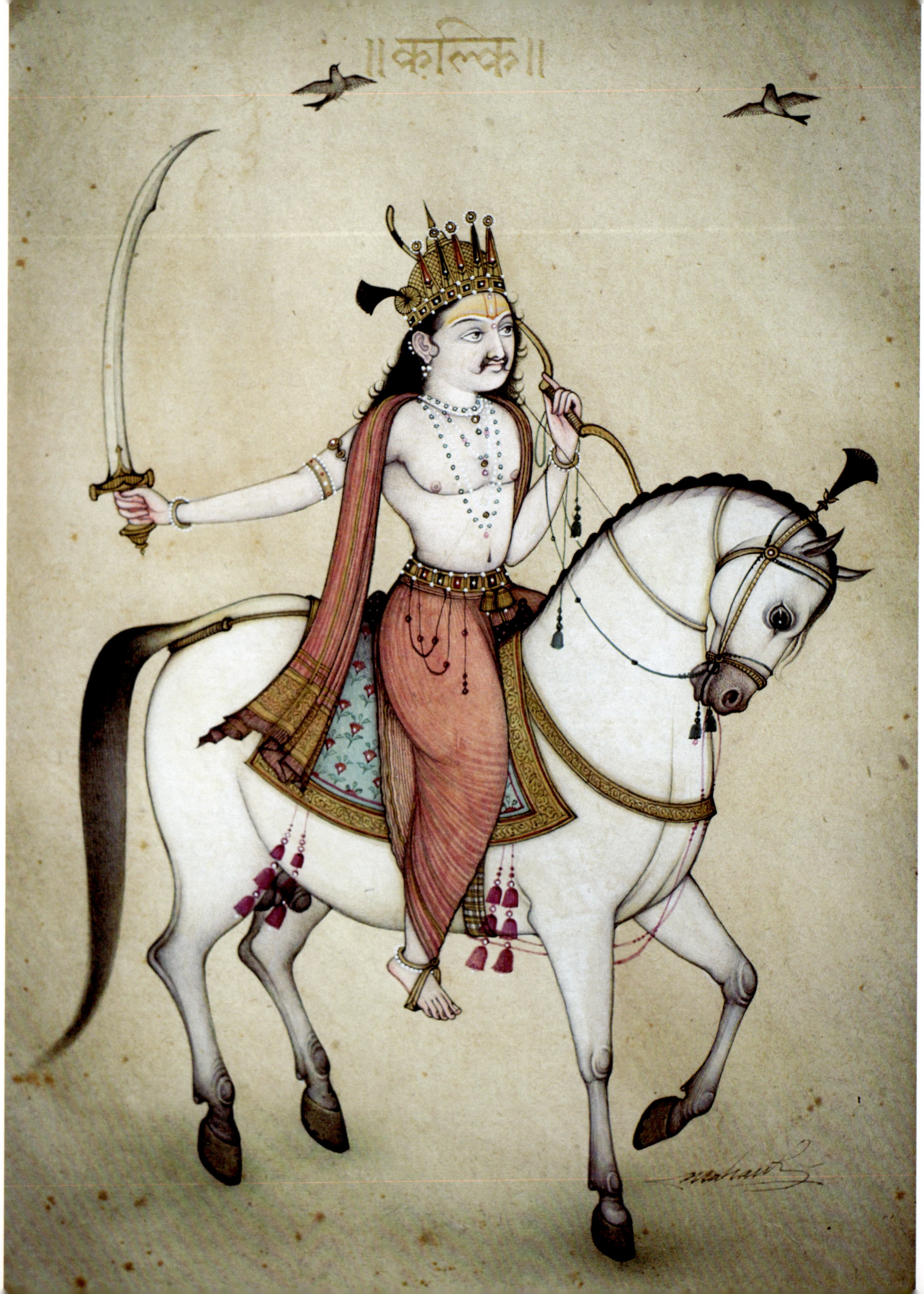
॥ कल्कि ॥

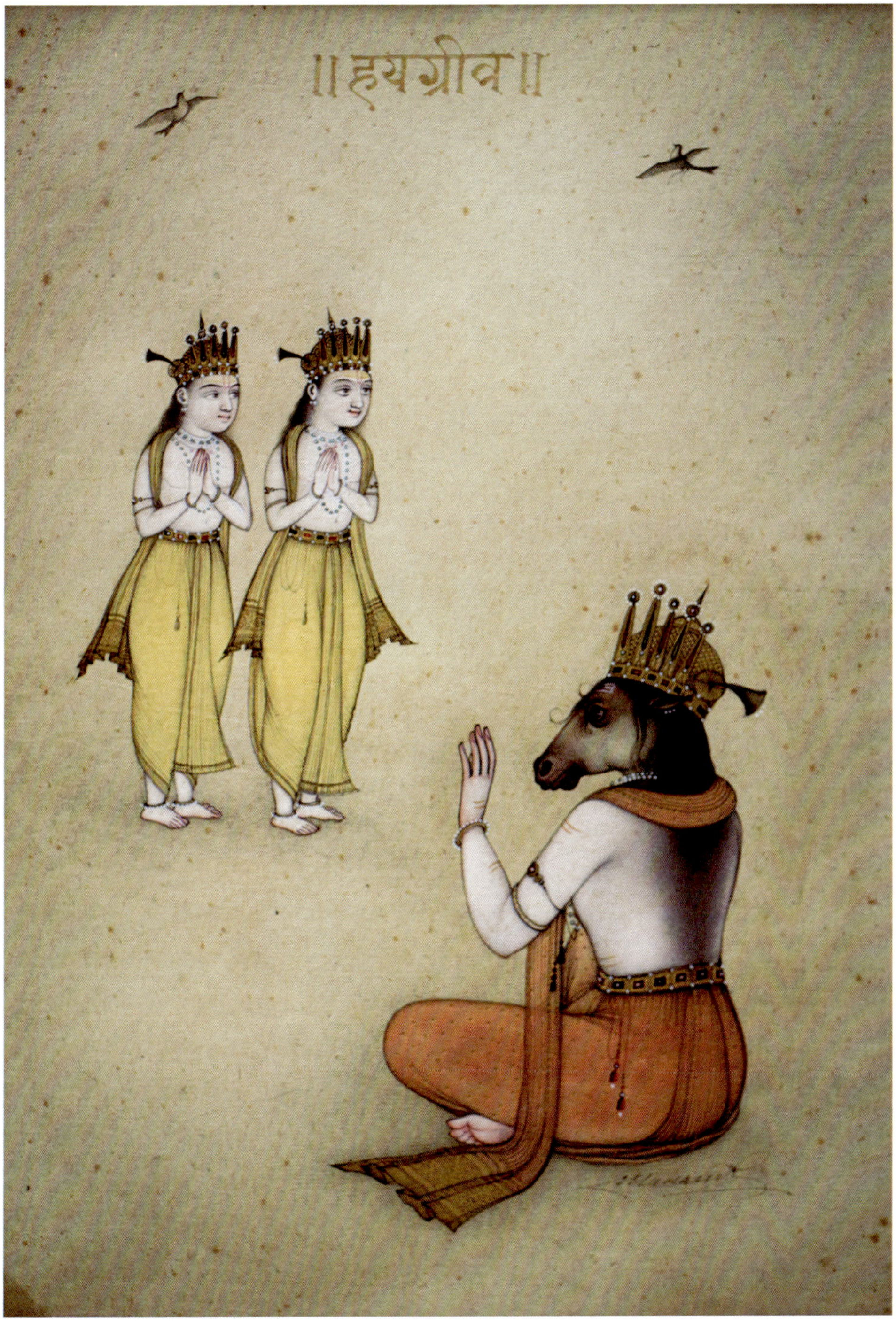

< Kalki
Natural pigments on handmade paper, 23x13cm

∧ Hayagriva
Natural pigments on handmade paper, 23x13cm

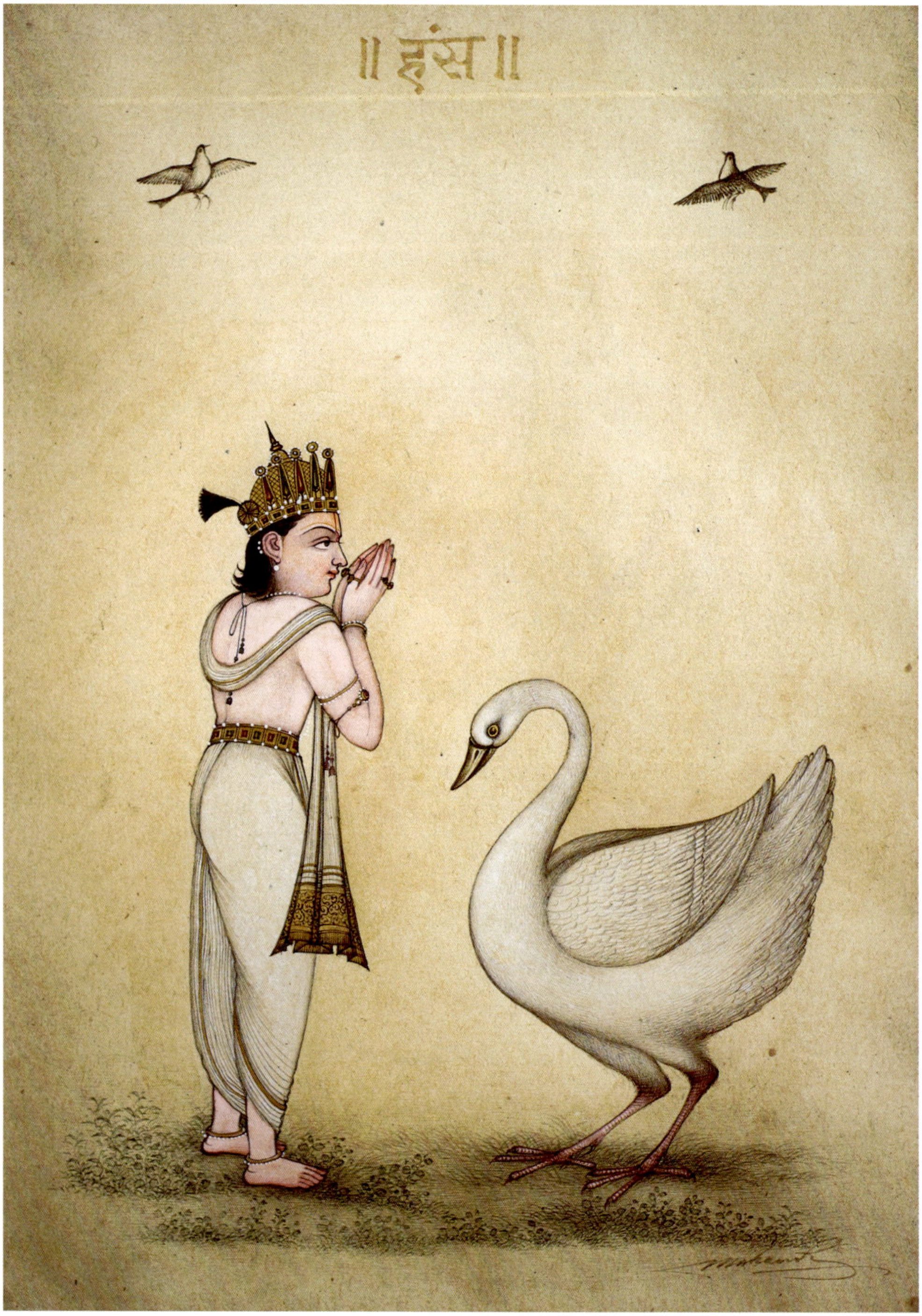

Hamsa
Natural pigments on handmade paper, 23x13cm

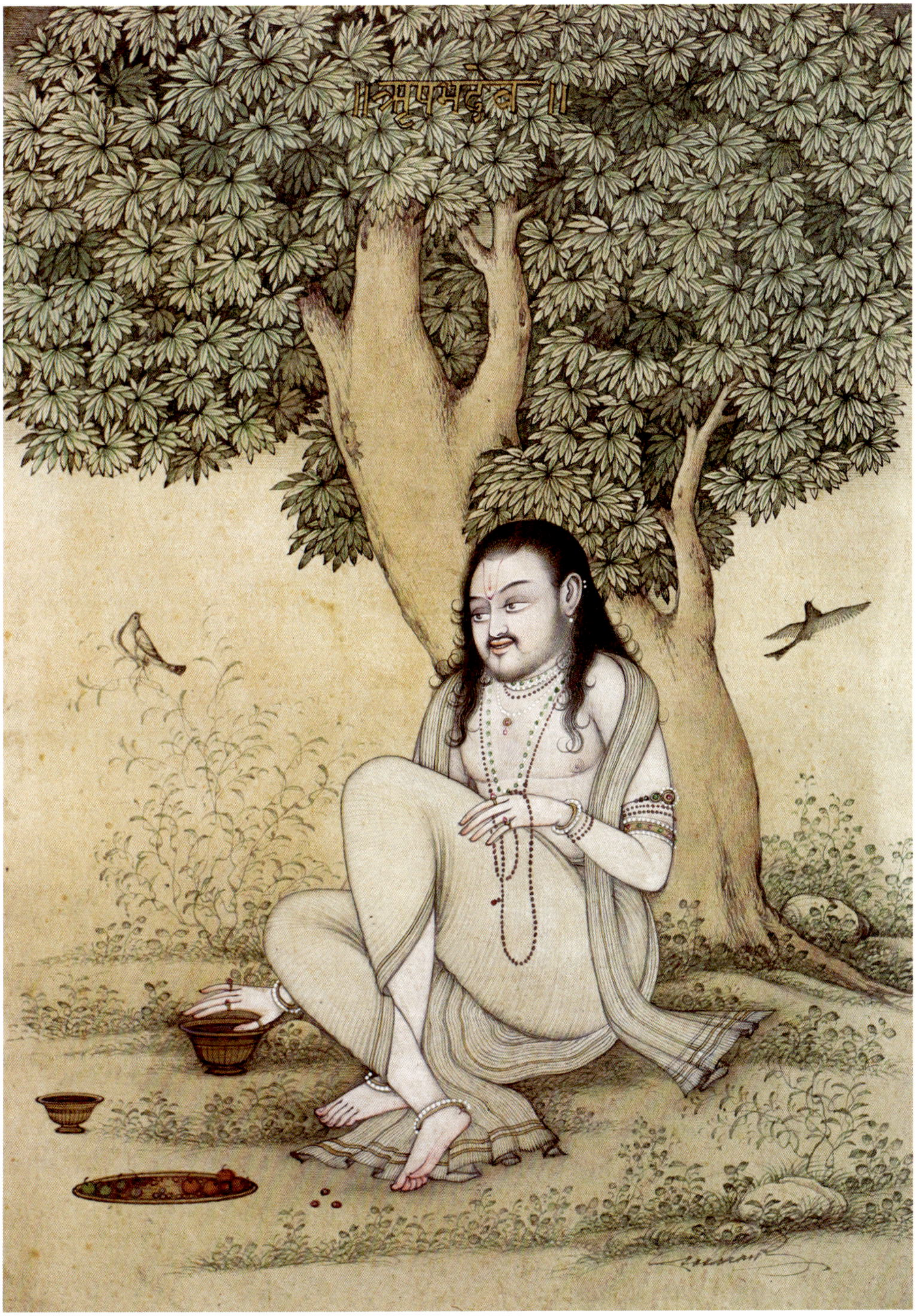

Rsabhadev
Natural pigments on handmade paper, 23x13cm

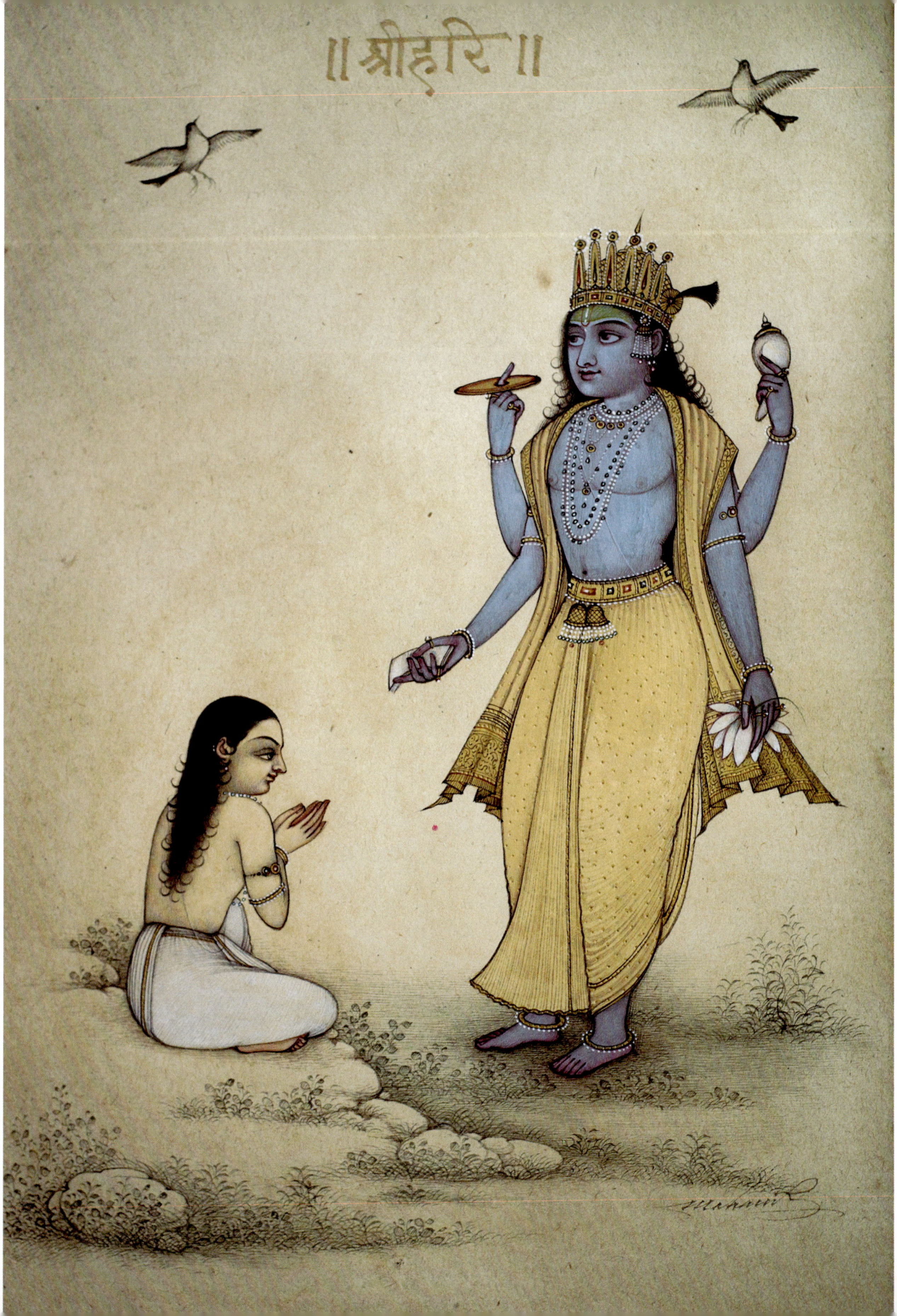
॥ श्रीहरि ॥

< Dhruva
Natural pigments on handmade paper, 23x13cm

HANUMAN

Hanuman sitting on lotus >
Natural pigments on handmade paper, 23x19cm

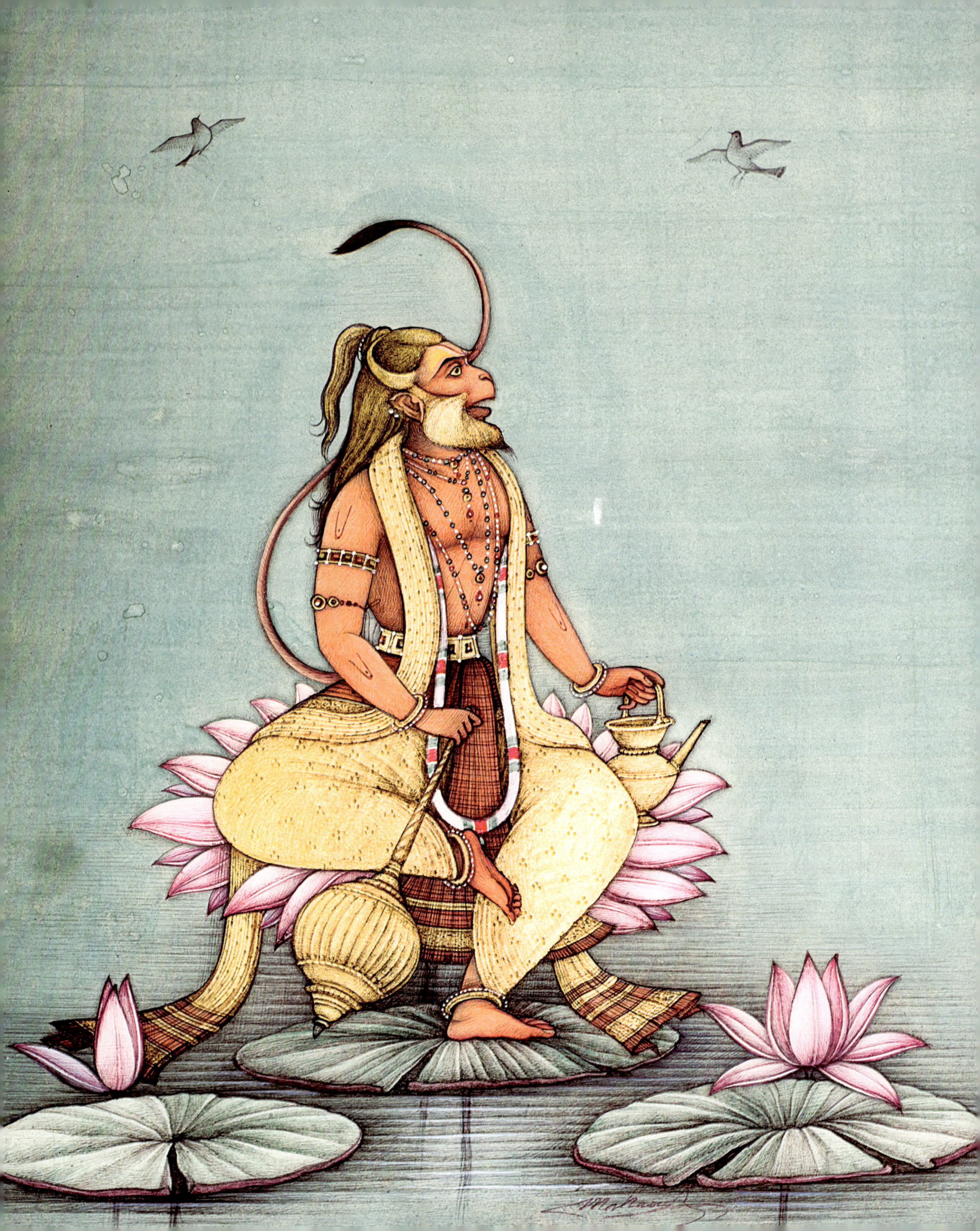

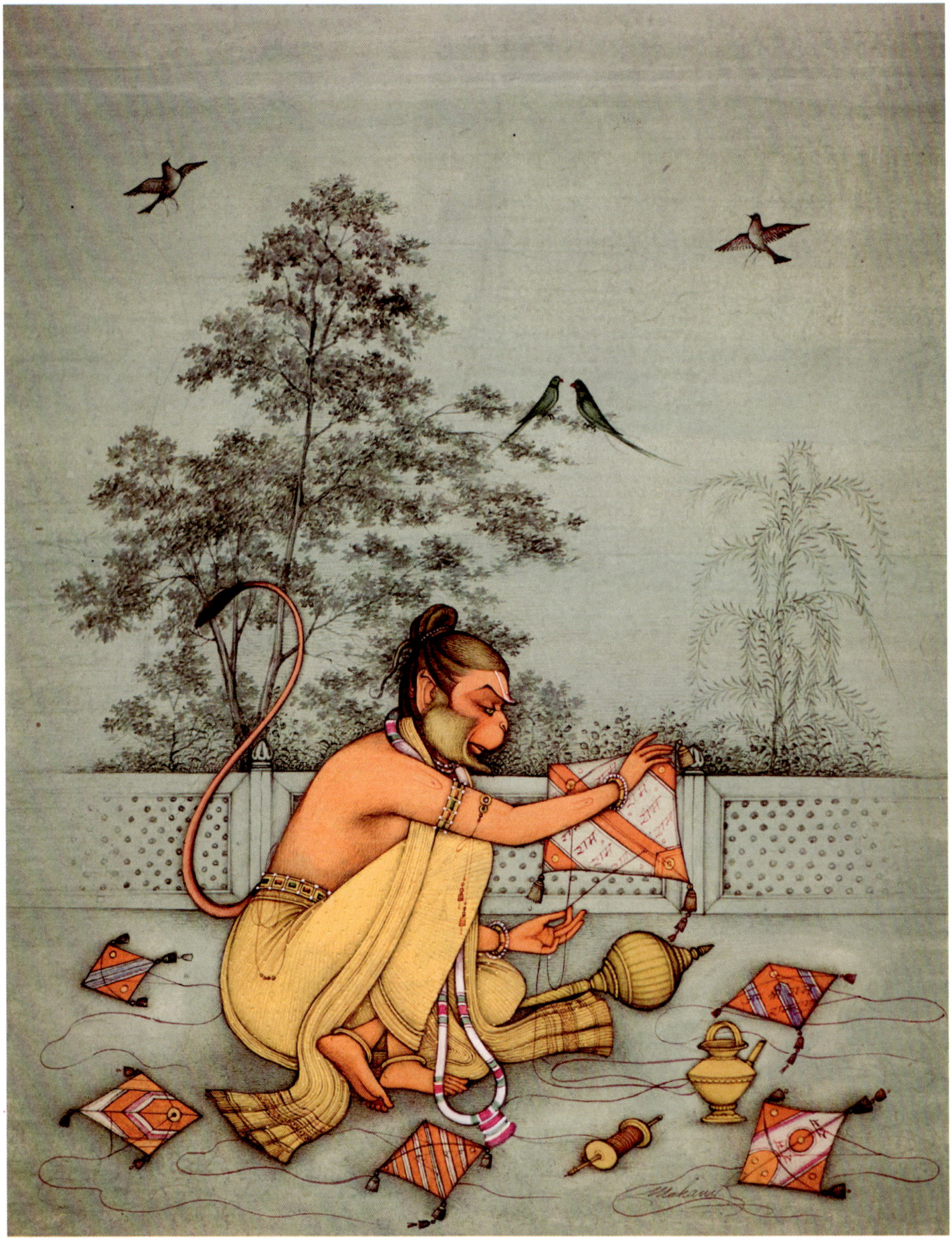

∧ Hanuman making kites
Natural pigments on handmade paper, 23x19cm

Hanuman dancing >
Natural pigments on handmade paper, 23x19cm

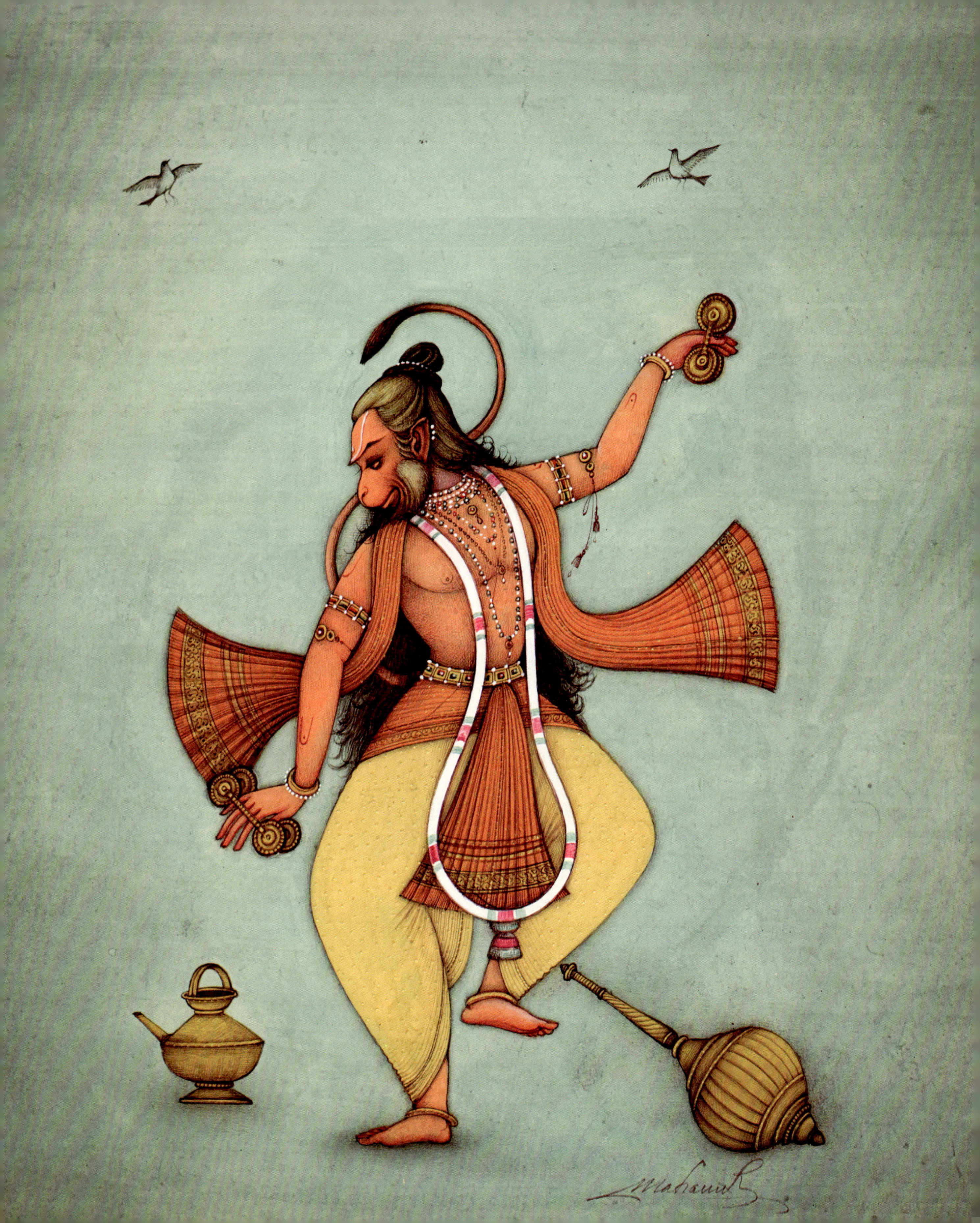

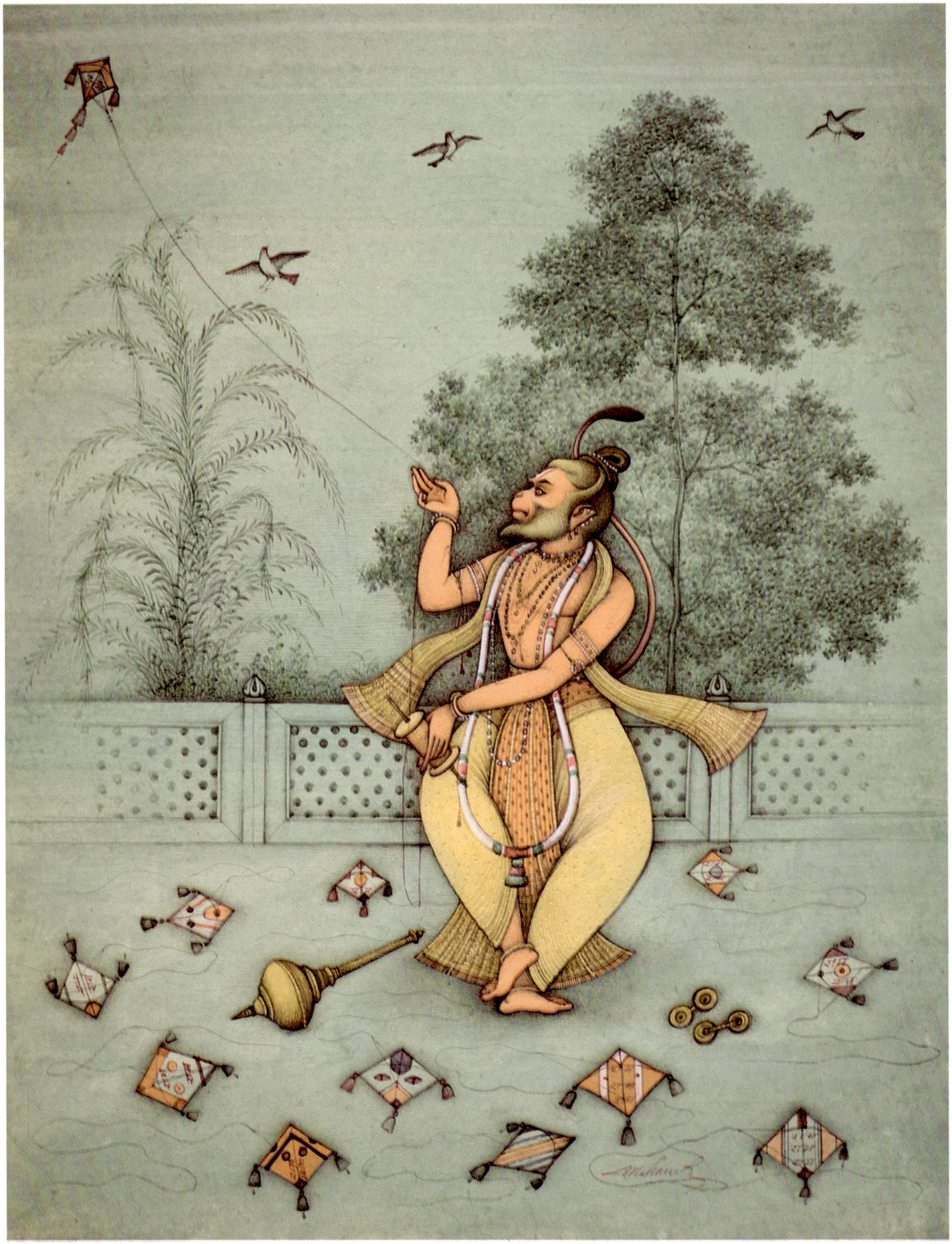

∧ Hanuman flying kite
Natural pigments on handmade paper, 23x19cm

Virat Hanuman >
Natural pigments on handmade paper, 38x24cm

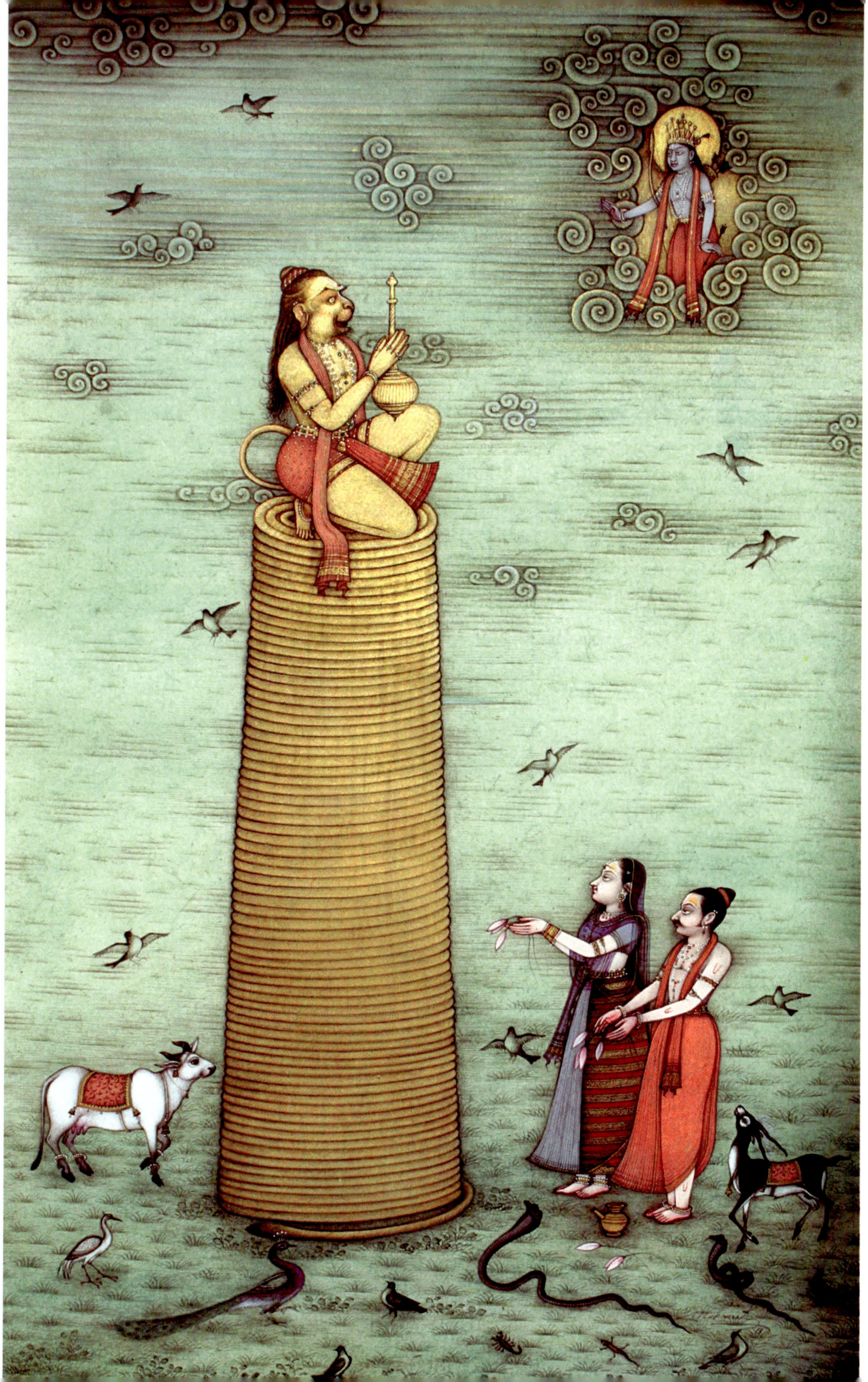

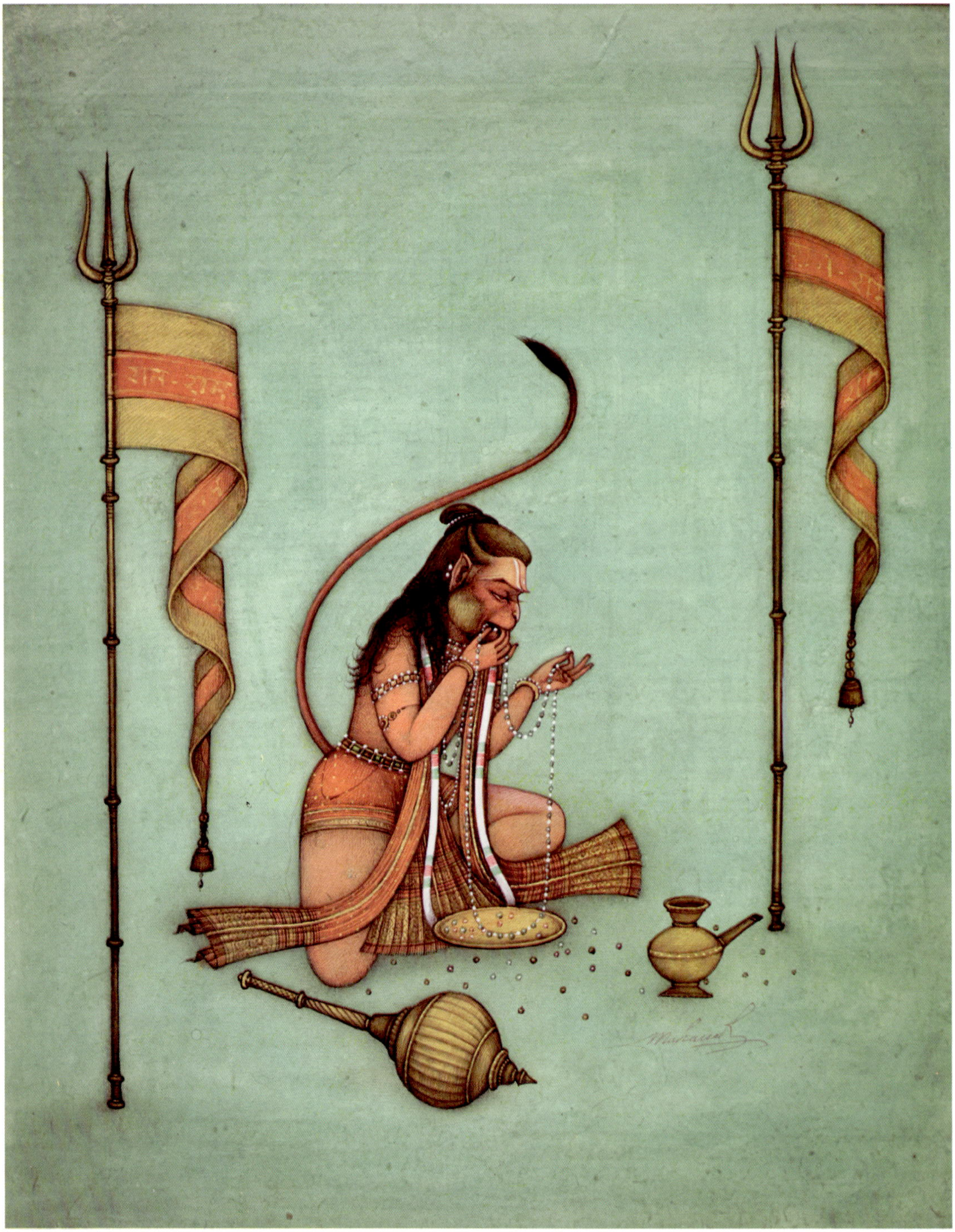

∧ Hanuman with beads
Natural pigments on handmade paper, 61.5x30.5cm

Hanuman Holding a Flag >
Natural pigments on handmade paper, 23x18cm

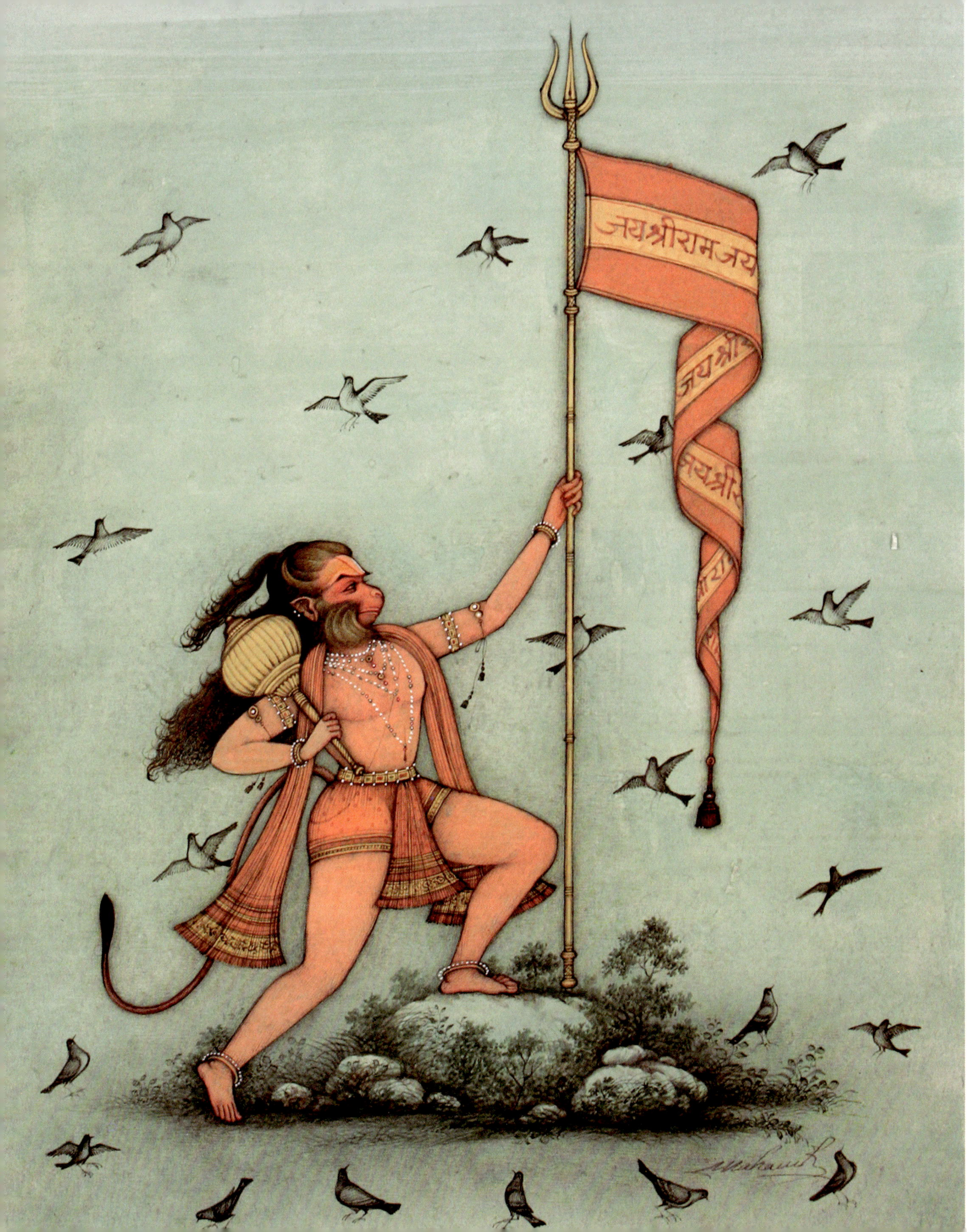
जयश्रीरामजय

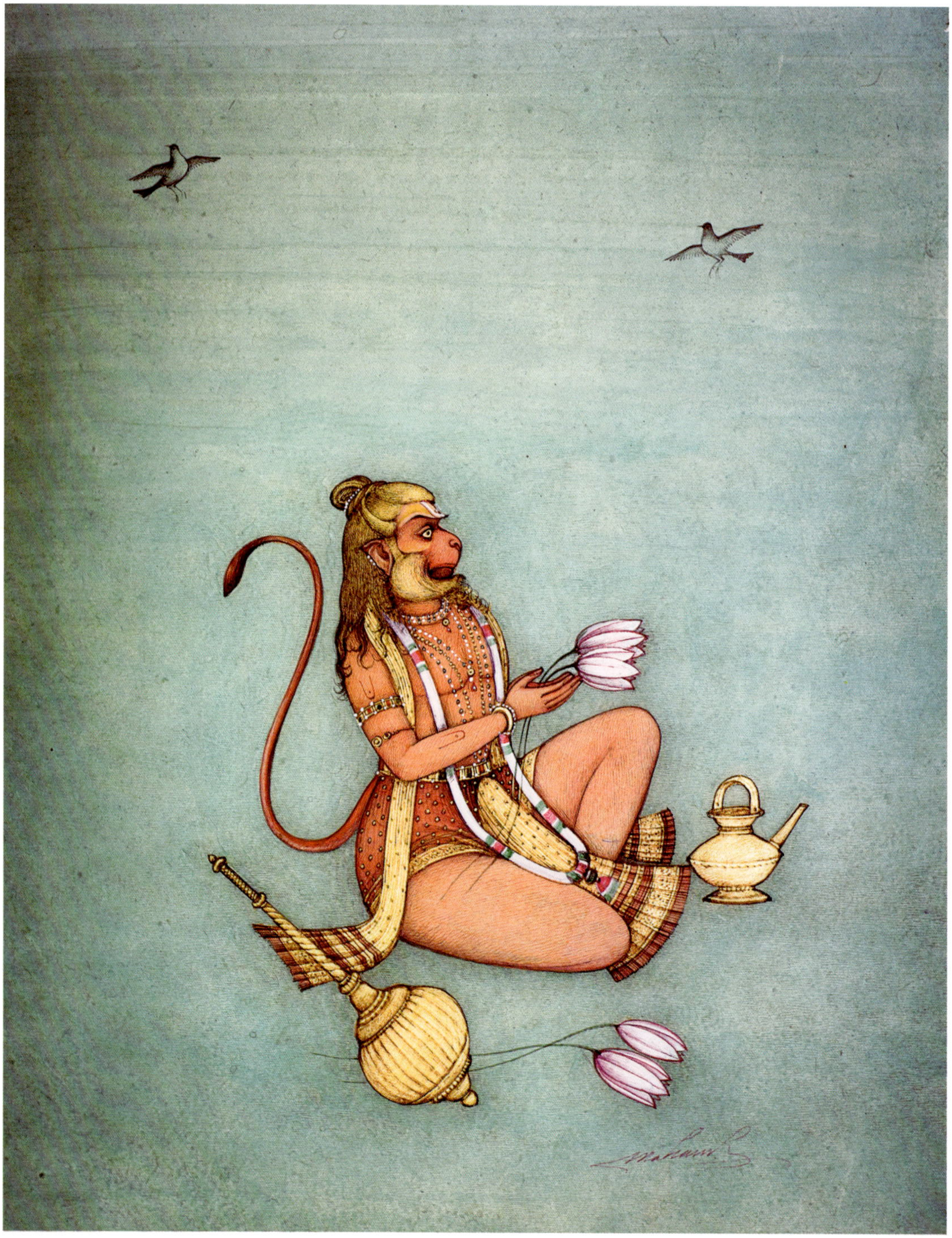

∧ Hanuman Lotuses
Natural pigments on handmade paper, 23x18cm

Hanuman with Gada and Shield >
Natural pigments on handmade paper, 23x18cm

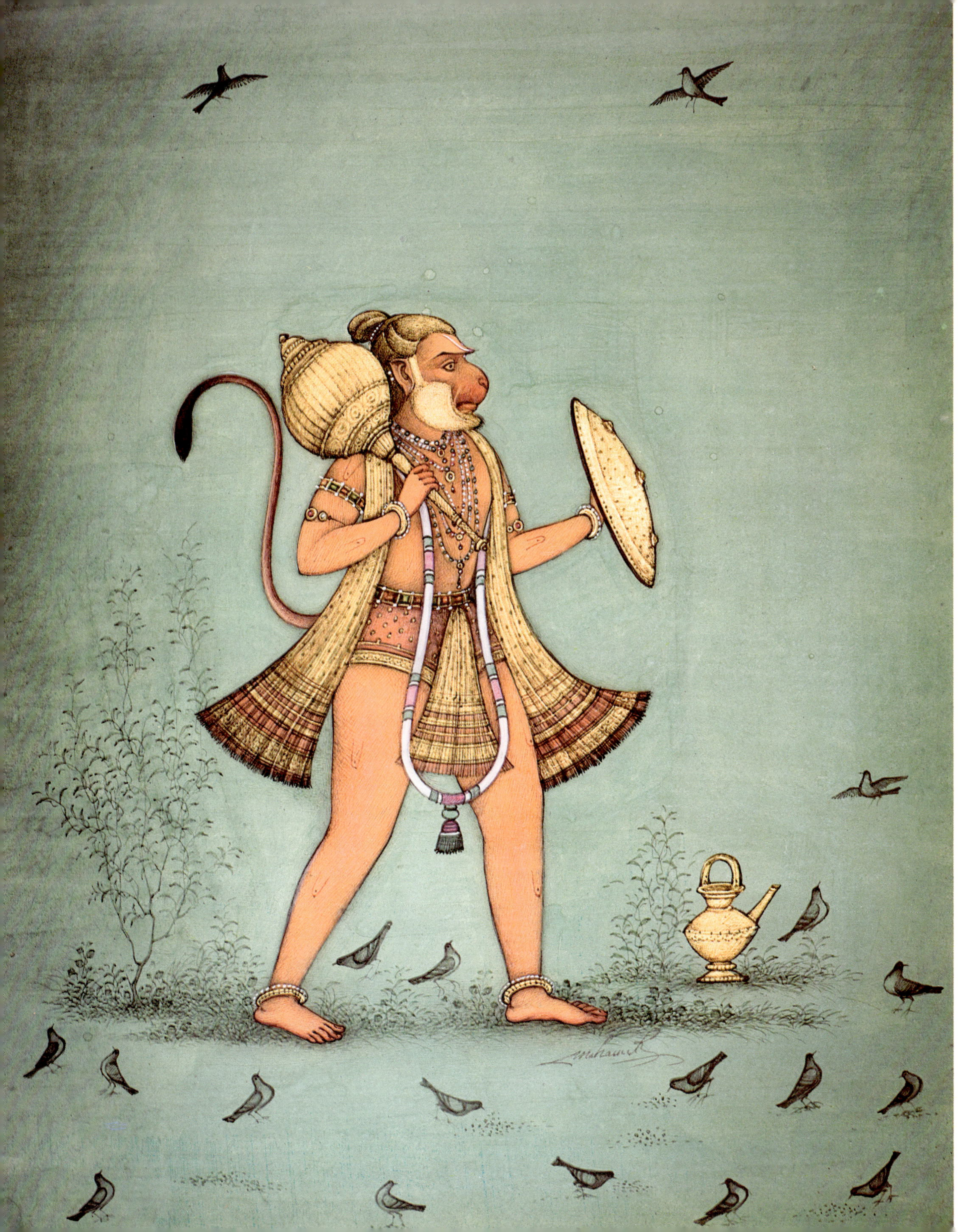

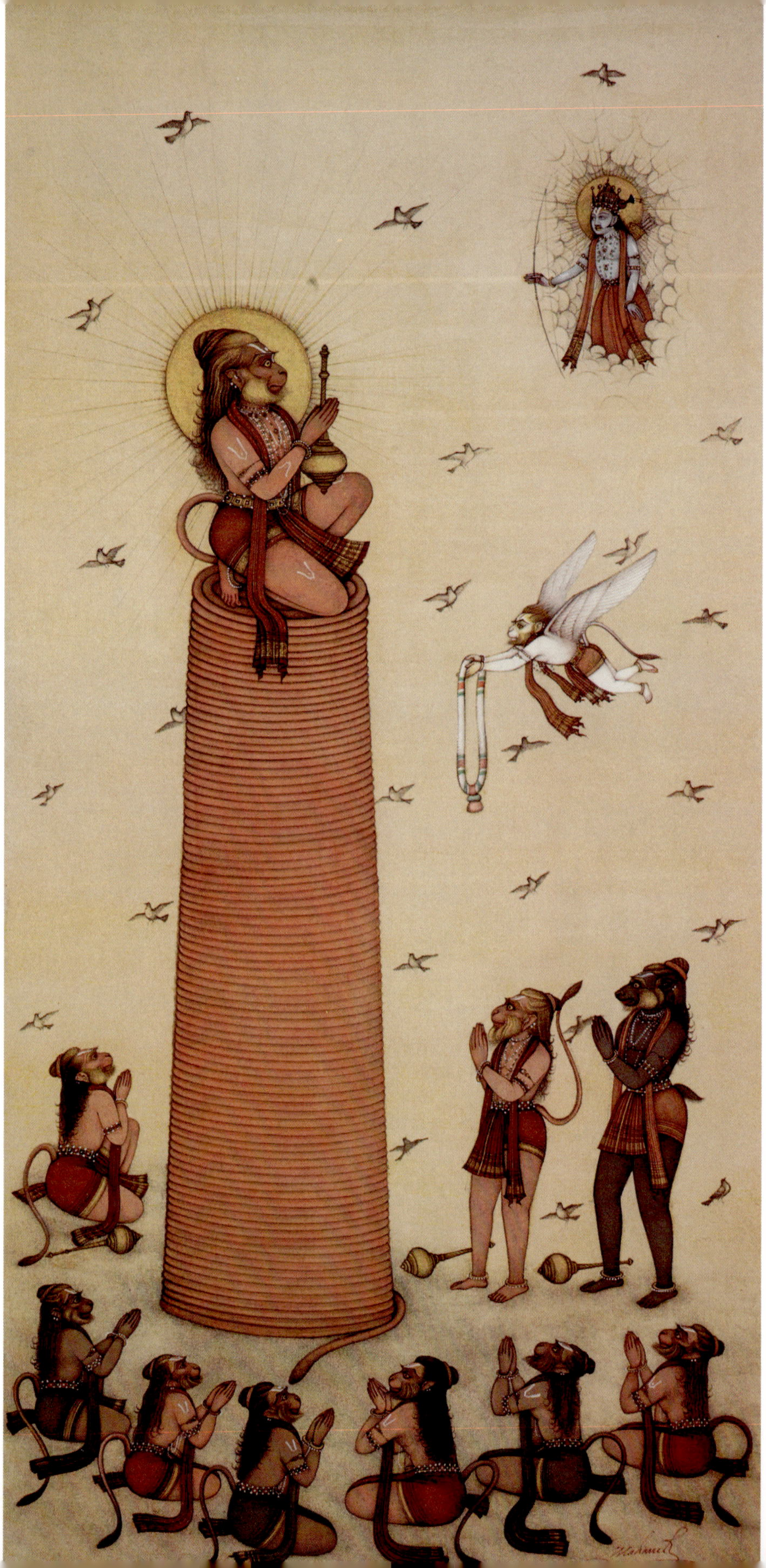

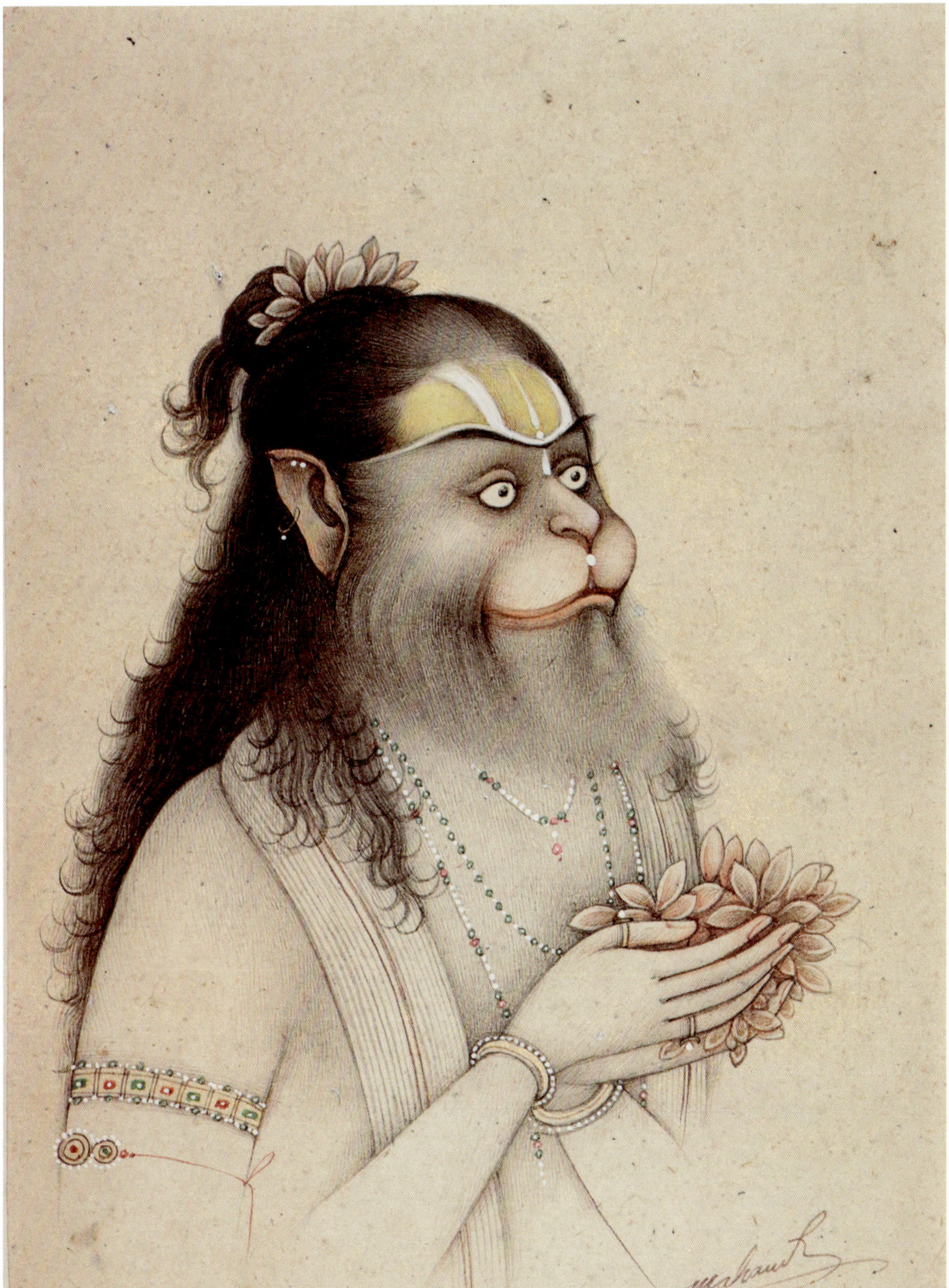

<Virat Hanuman
Natural pigments on pure silk, 61.5x30.5cm

∧ Hanuman Head
Natural pigments on handmade paper, 16x12cm

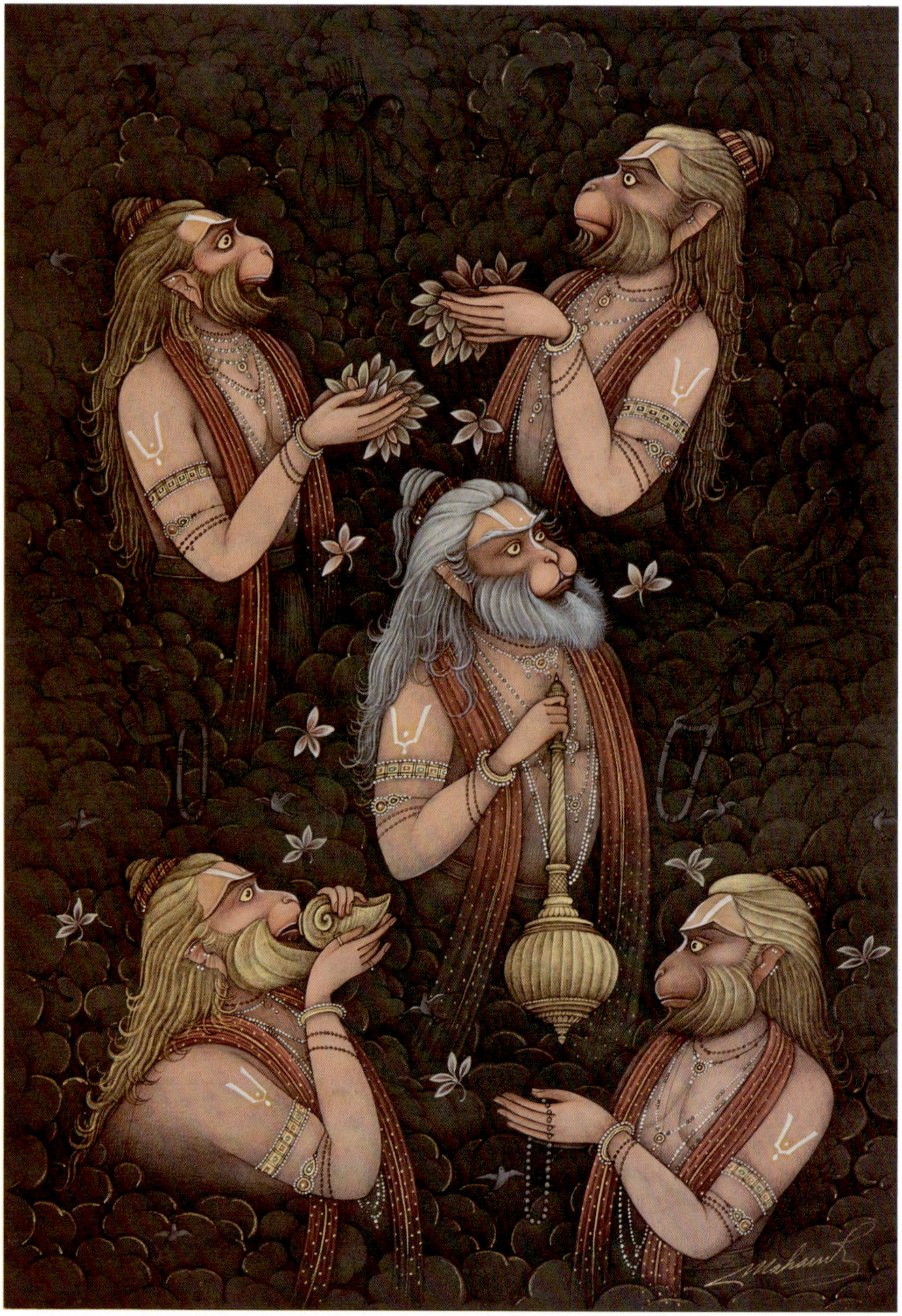

Hanuman Rupas
Natural pigments on handmade paper, 51x41cm

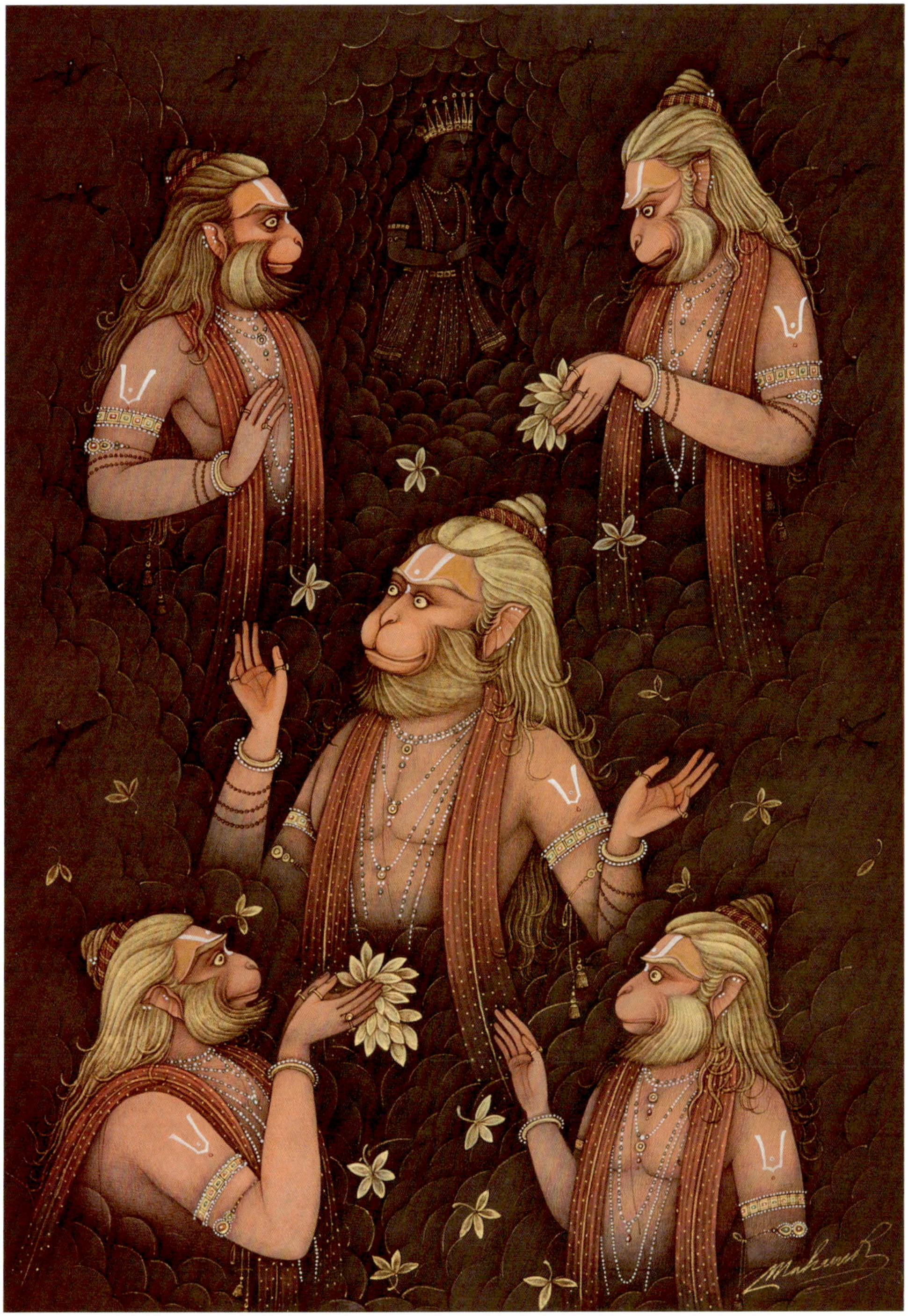

Hanuman Rupas
Natural pigments on handmade paper, 51x40cm

ASTA GANESHA

Ganesha on a snake >
Natural pigments on vasli, 23x13cm

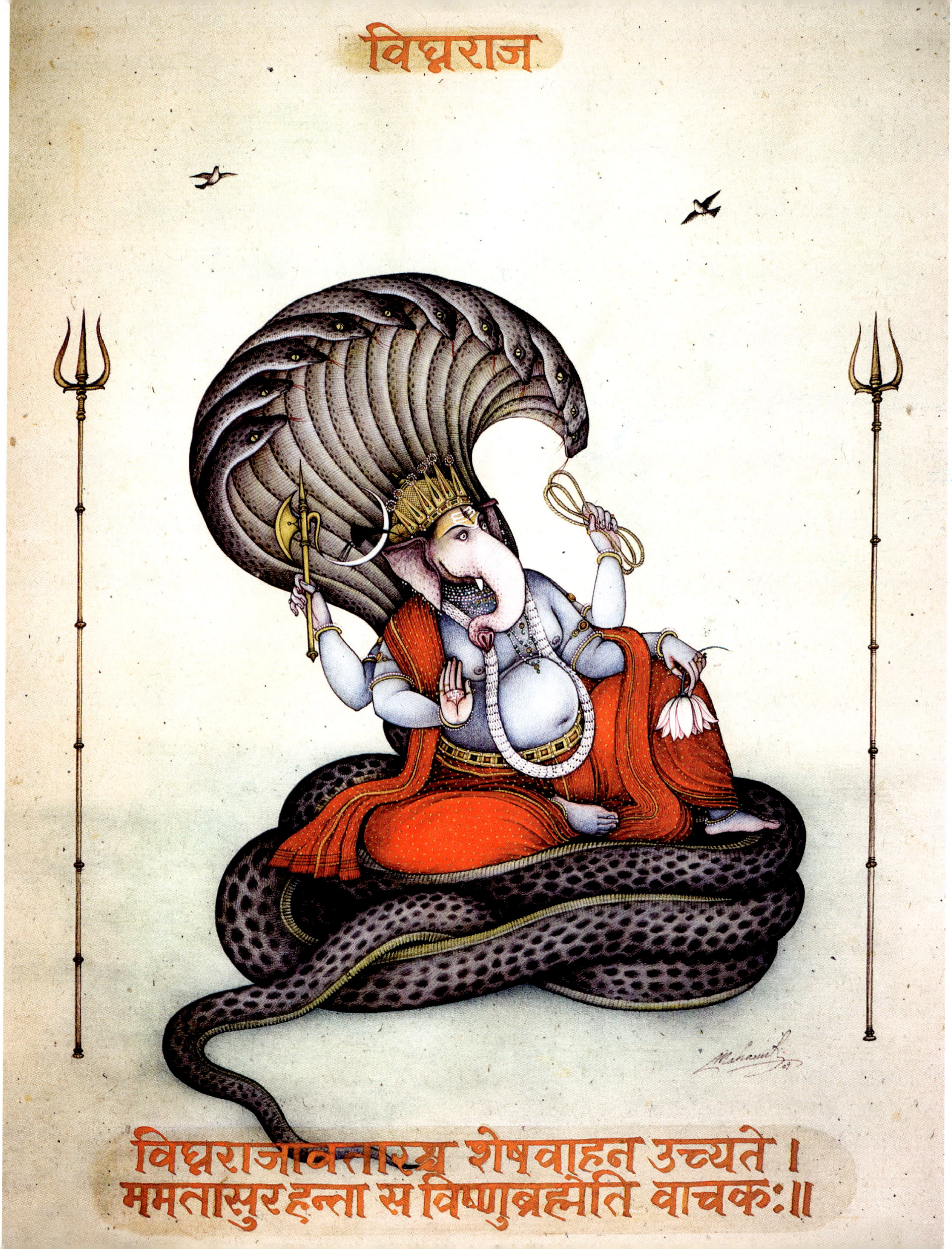
विघ्नराज
विघ्नराजावतारश्च शेषवाहन उच्यते ।
ममतासुरहन्ता स विष्णुब्रह्मेति वाचकः ॥

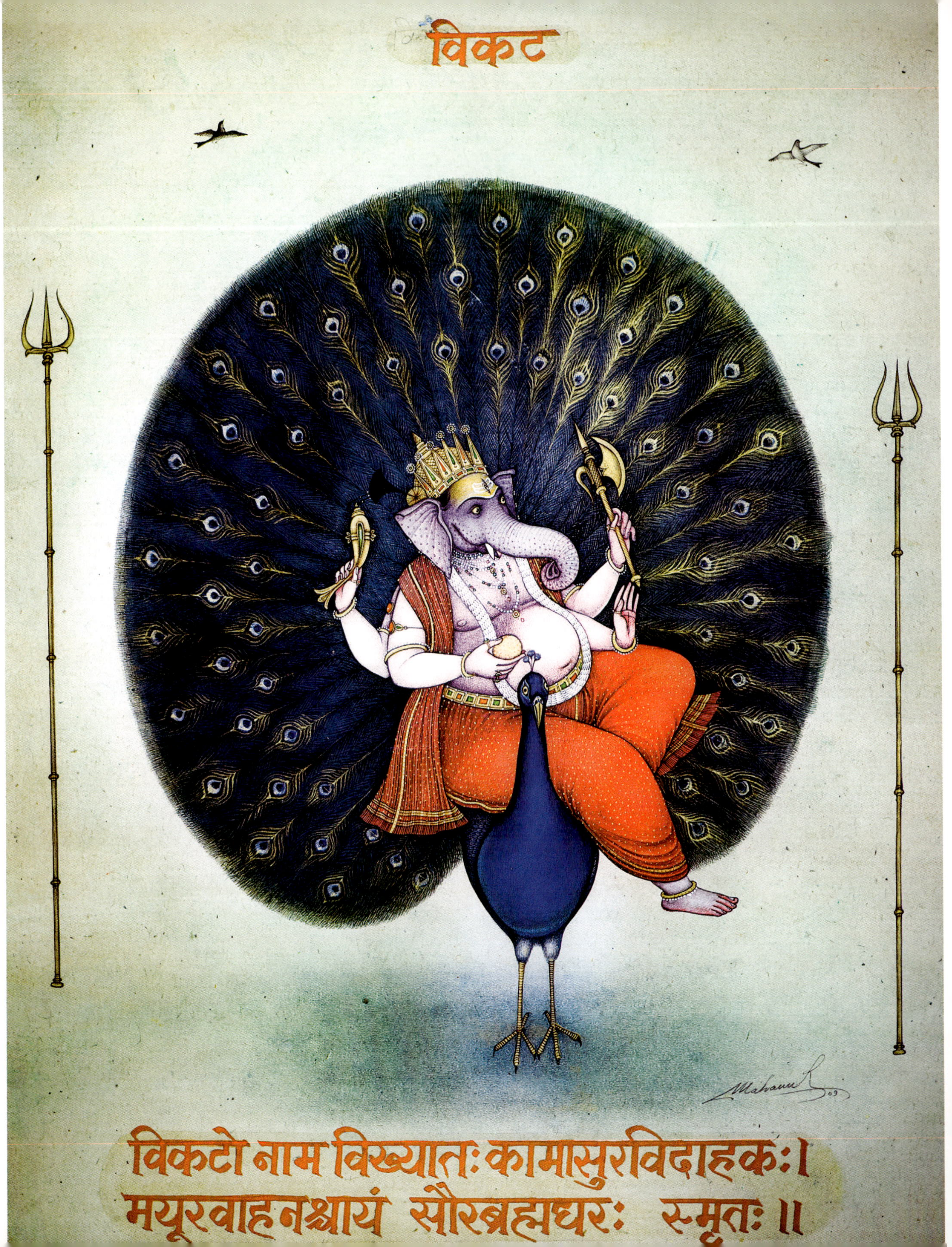
विकट
विकटो नाम विख्यातः कामासुरविदाहकः ।
मयूरवाहनश्चायं सौरब्रह्मधरः स्मृतः ॥

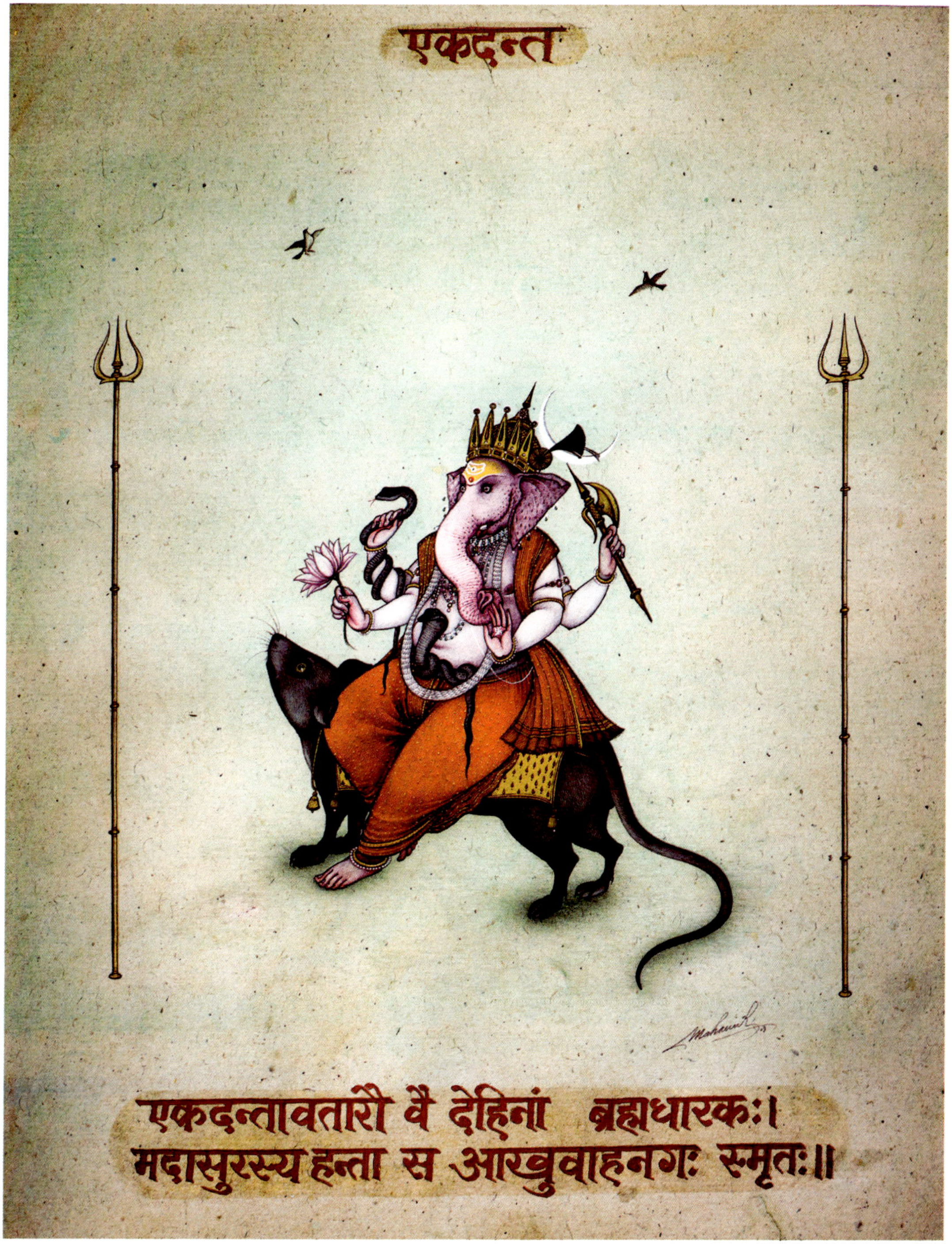

< Ganesha on peacock
Natural pigments on vasli, 43x34cm

∧ Ganesha on rat
Natural pigments on vasli, 43x34cm

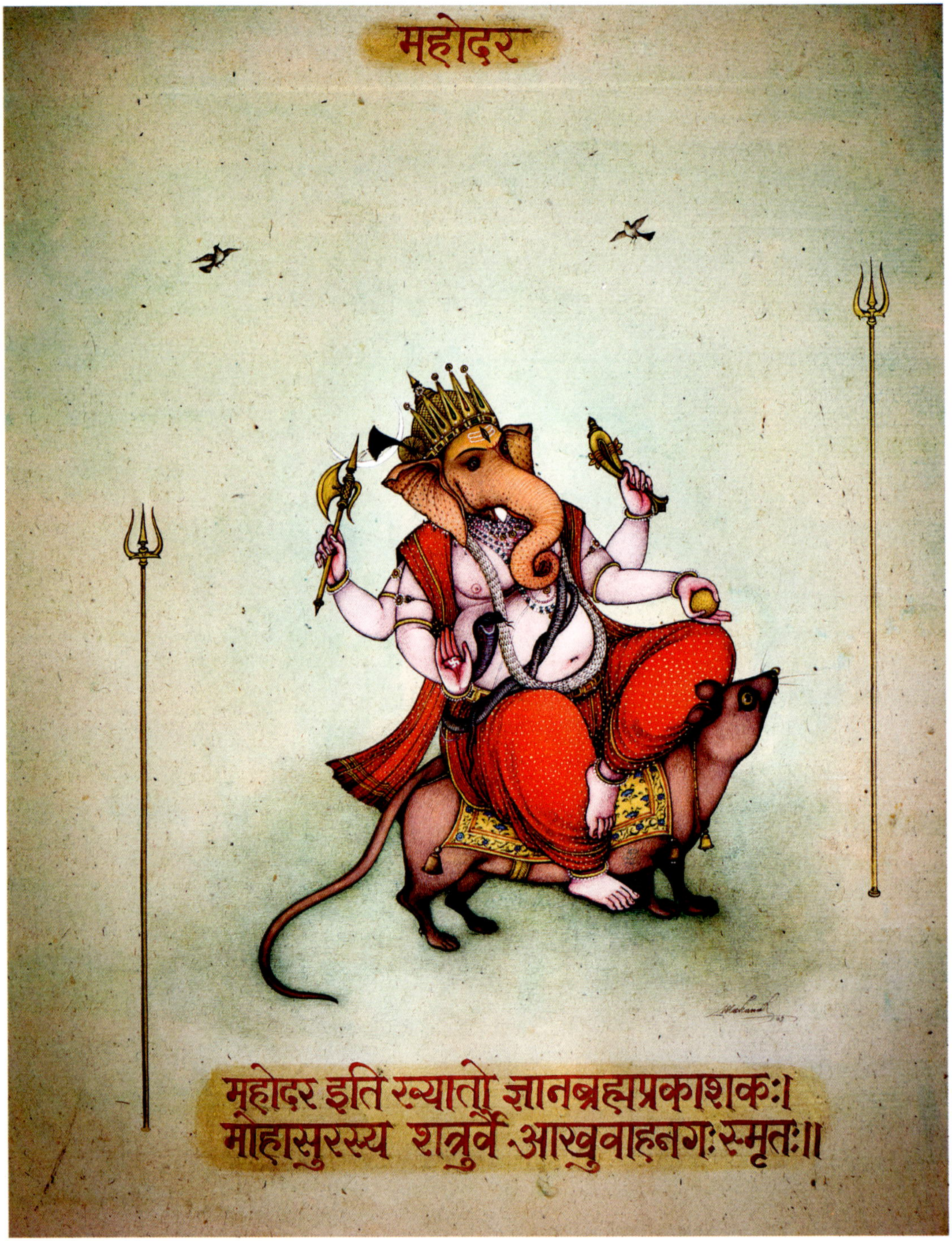

Ganesha on brown rat
Natural pigments on vasli, 43x34cm

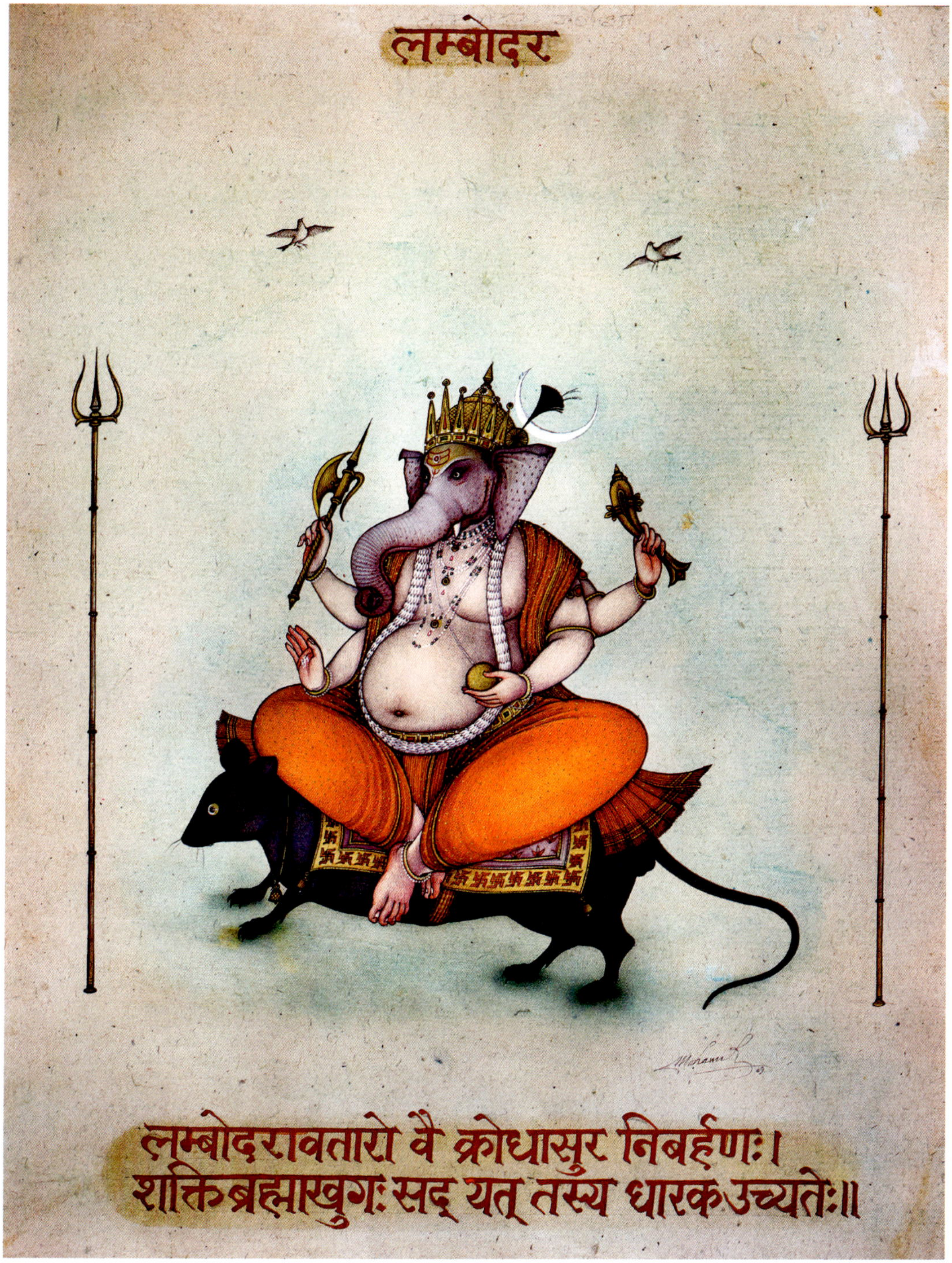

Ganesha on blue rat
Natural pigments on vasli, 43x34cm

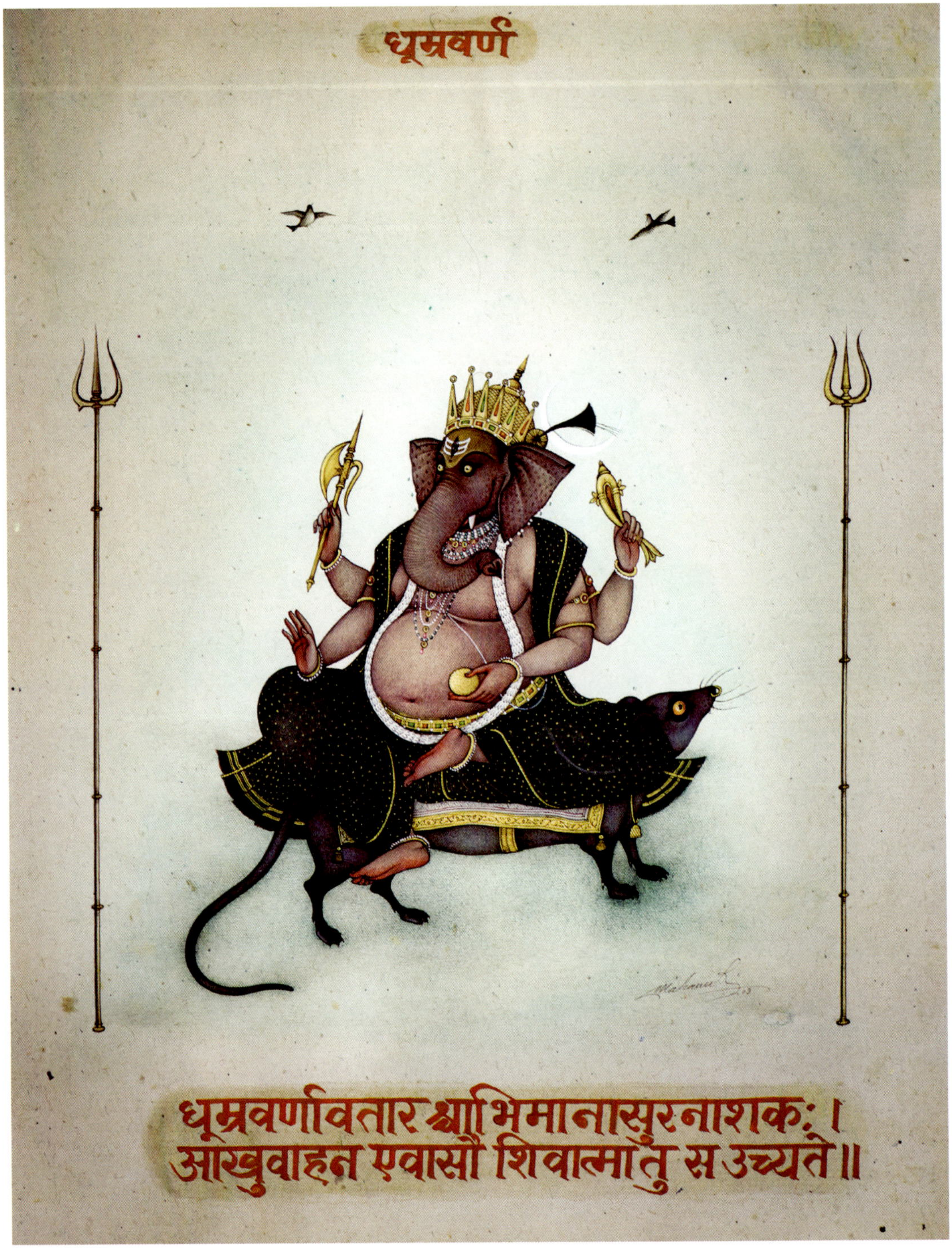

∧ Ganesha on black rat
Natural pigments on vasli, 43x34cm

Ganesha on white rat >
Natural pigments on vasli, 43x34cm

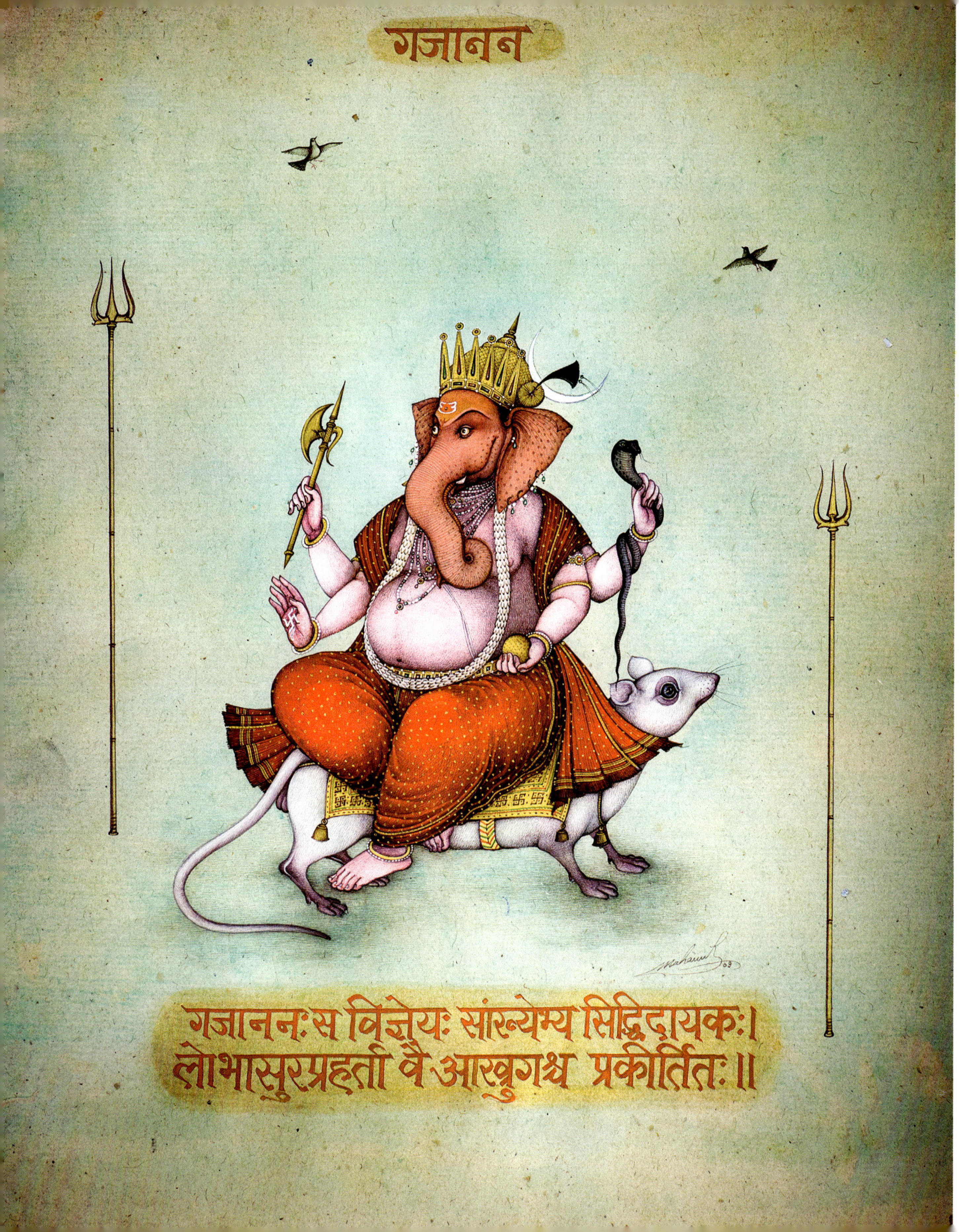
गजानन
गजाननःस विज्ञेयः सांख्येभ्य सिद्धिदायकः।
लोभासुरप्रहर्ता वै आखुगश्च प्रकीर्तितः॥

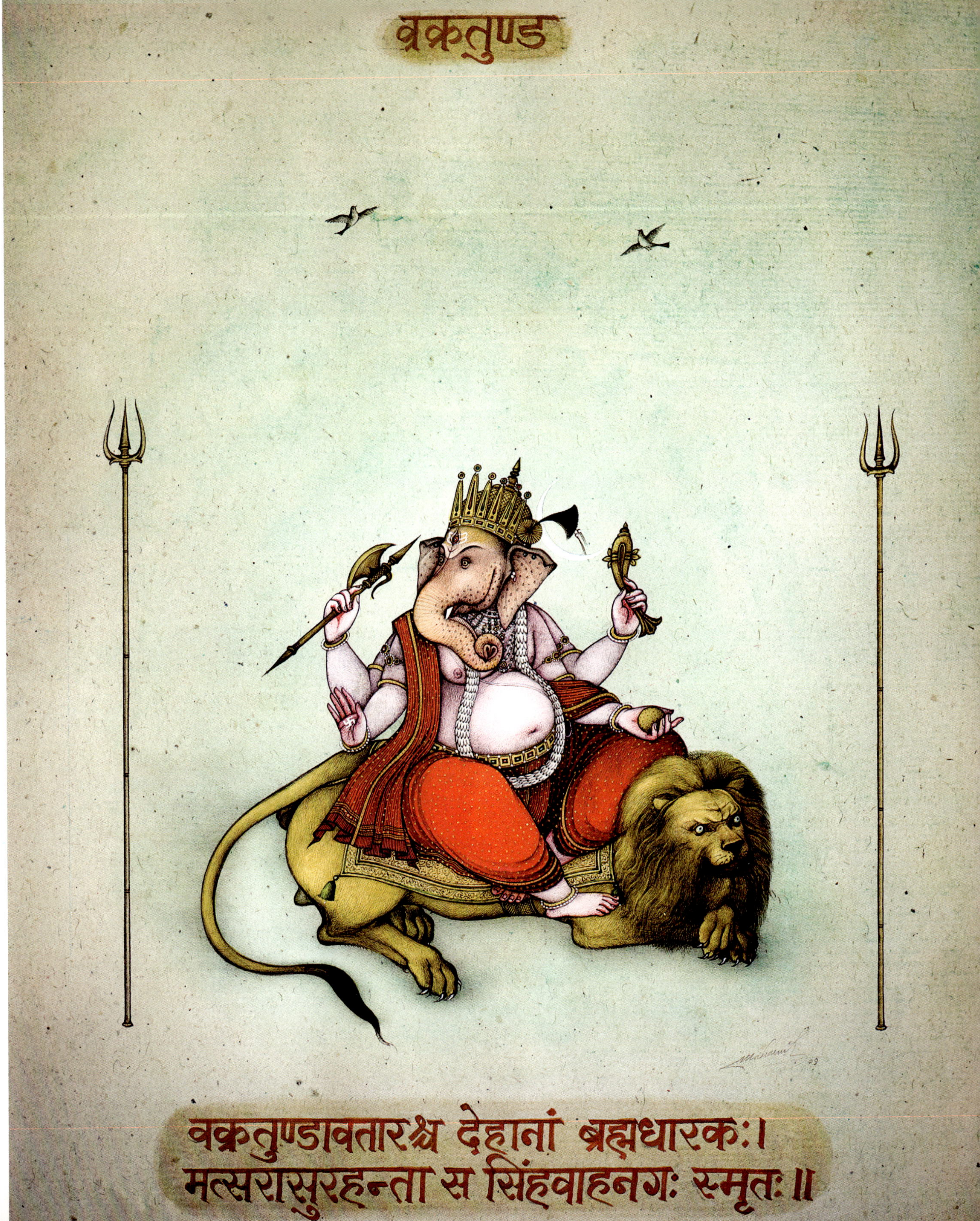
वक्रतुण्ड
वक्रतुण्डावतारश्च देहानां ब्रह्मधारकः।
मत्सरासुरहन्ता स सिंहवाहनगः स्मृतः॥

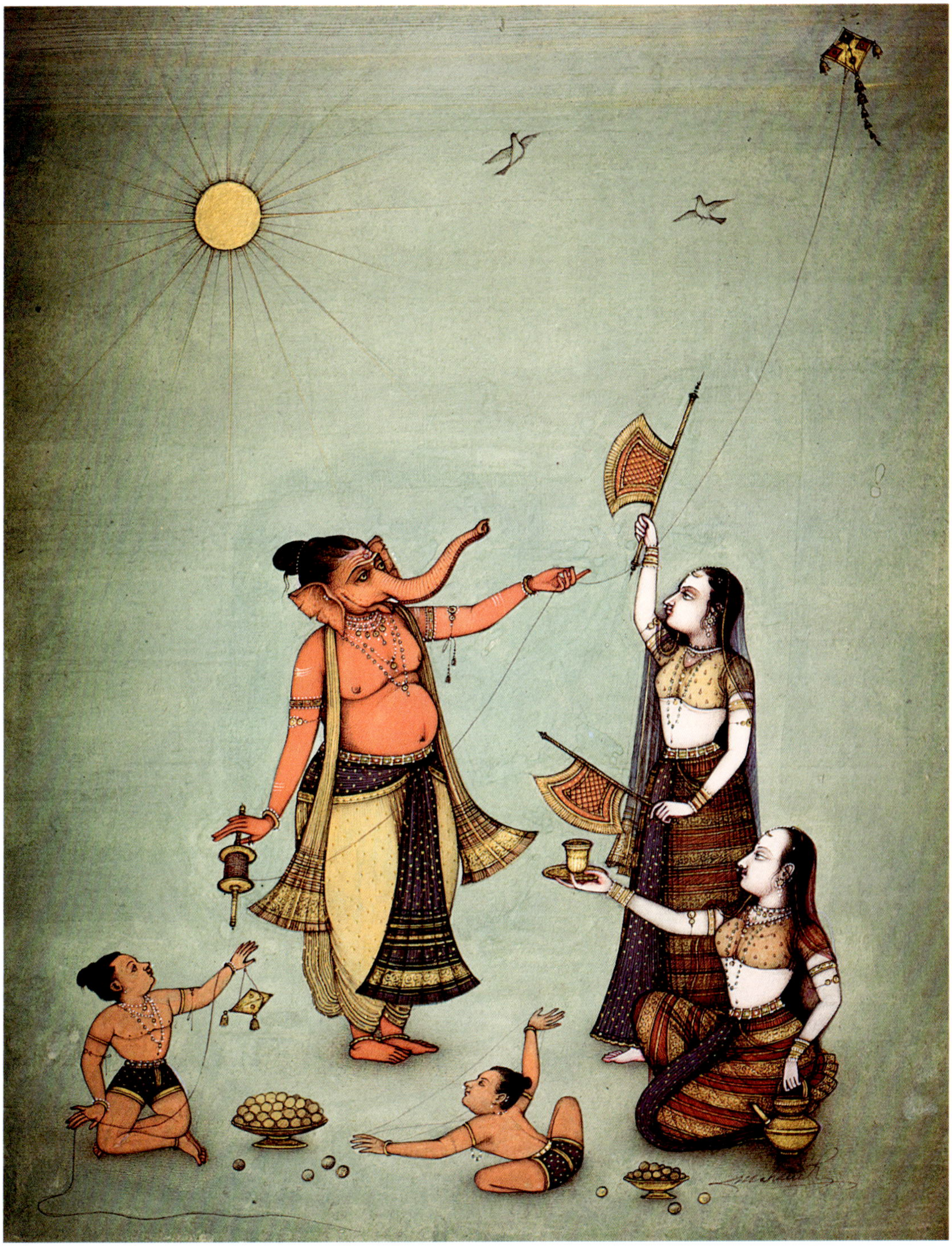

< Ganesha on a lion
Natural pigments on vasli, 43x34cm

∧ Ganesh and his family
Natural pigments on pure silk, 29x24cm

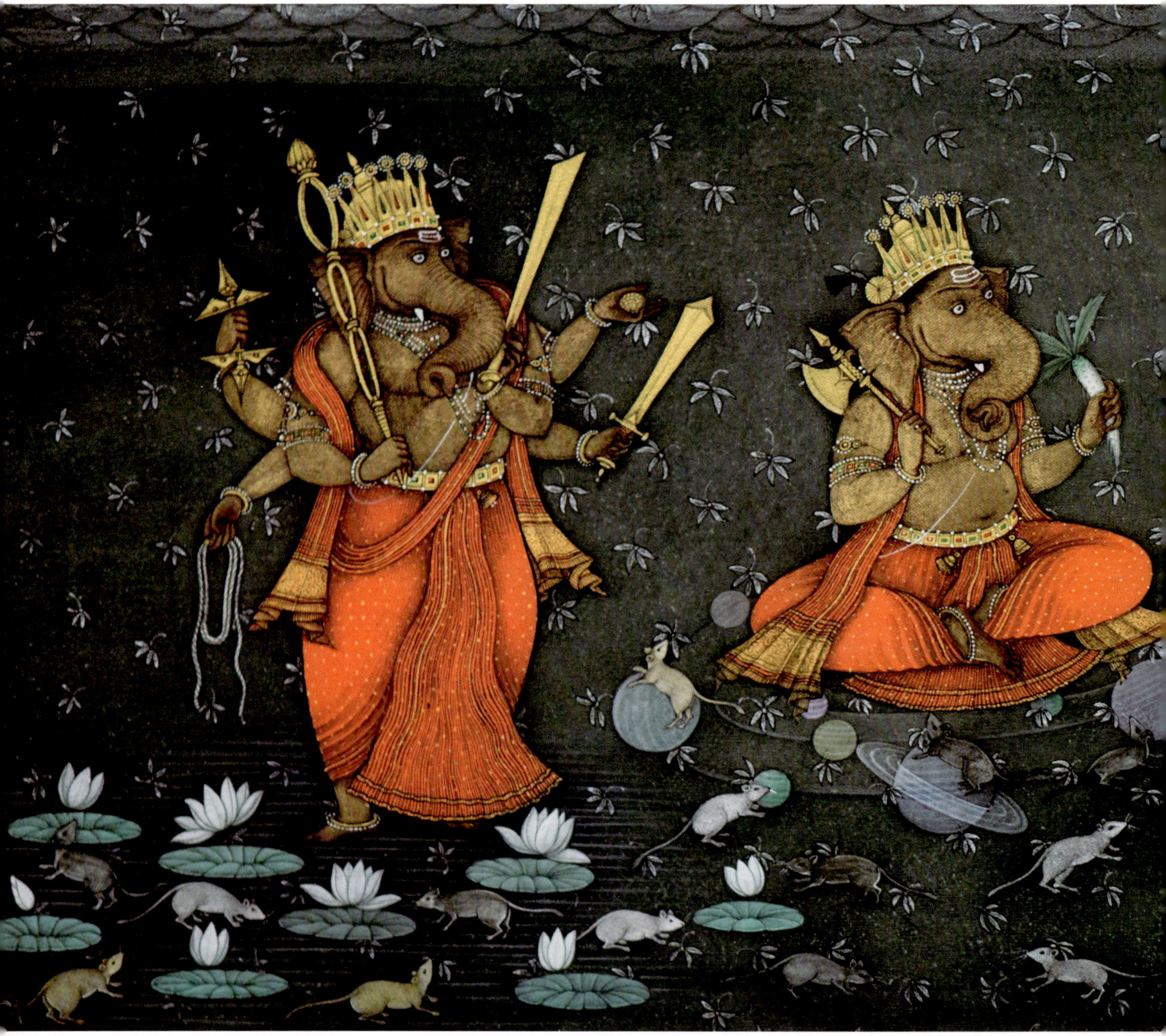

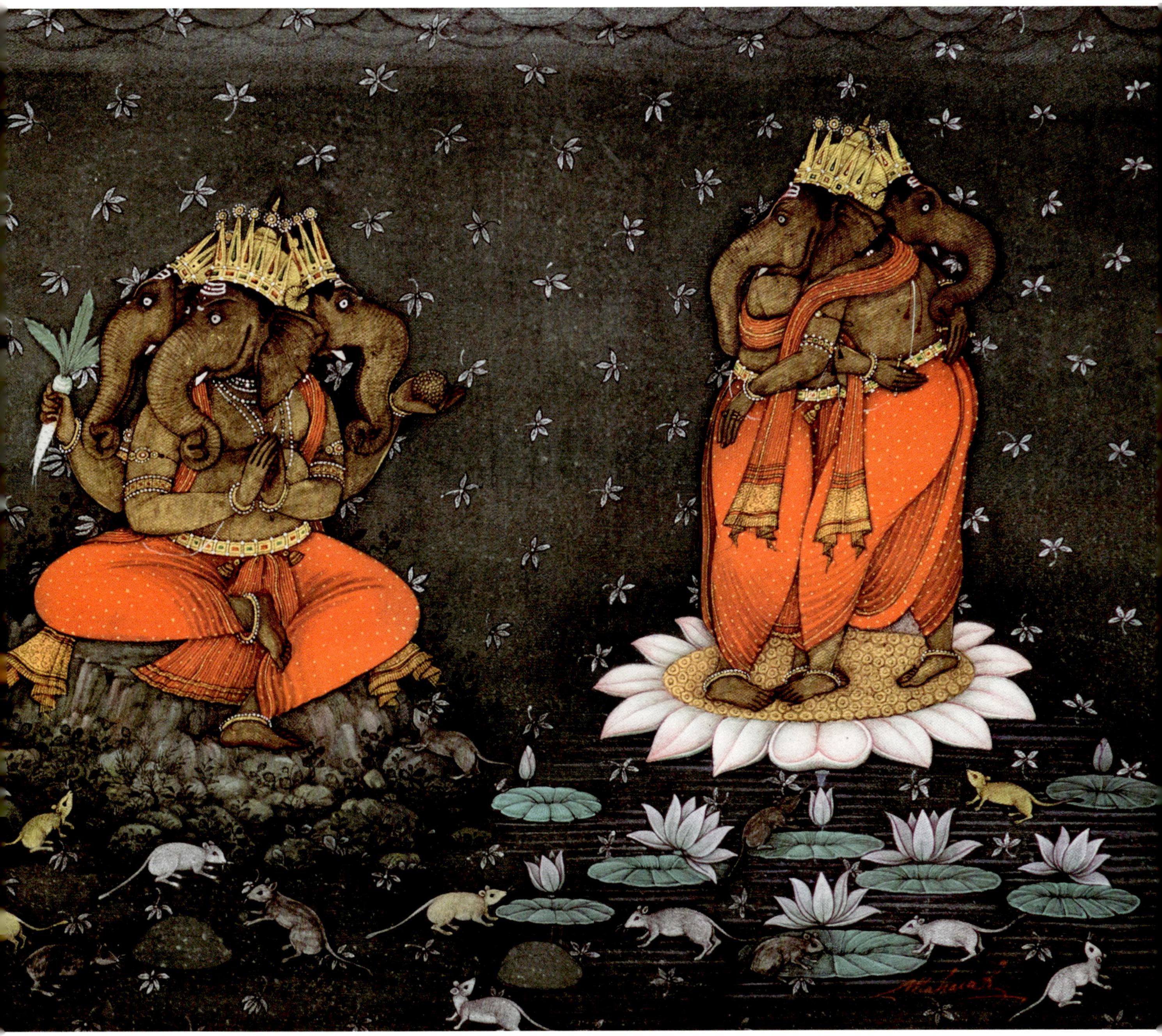

Ganesha (Four Rupas)
Pigments on paper, 52x21cm

SPIRITUAL INDIA

Ram and Sita with Laxman flying kite >
Natural pigments on pure silk

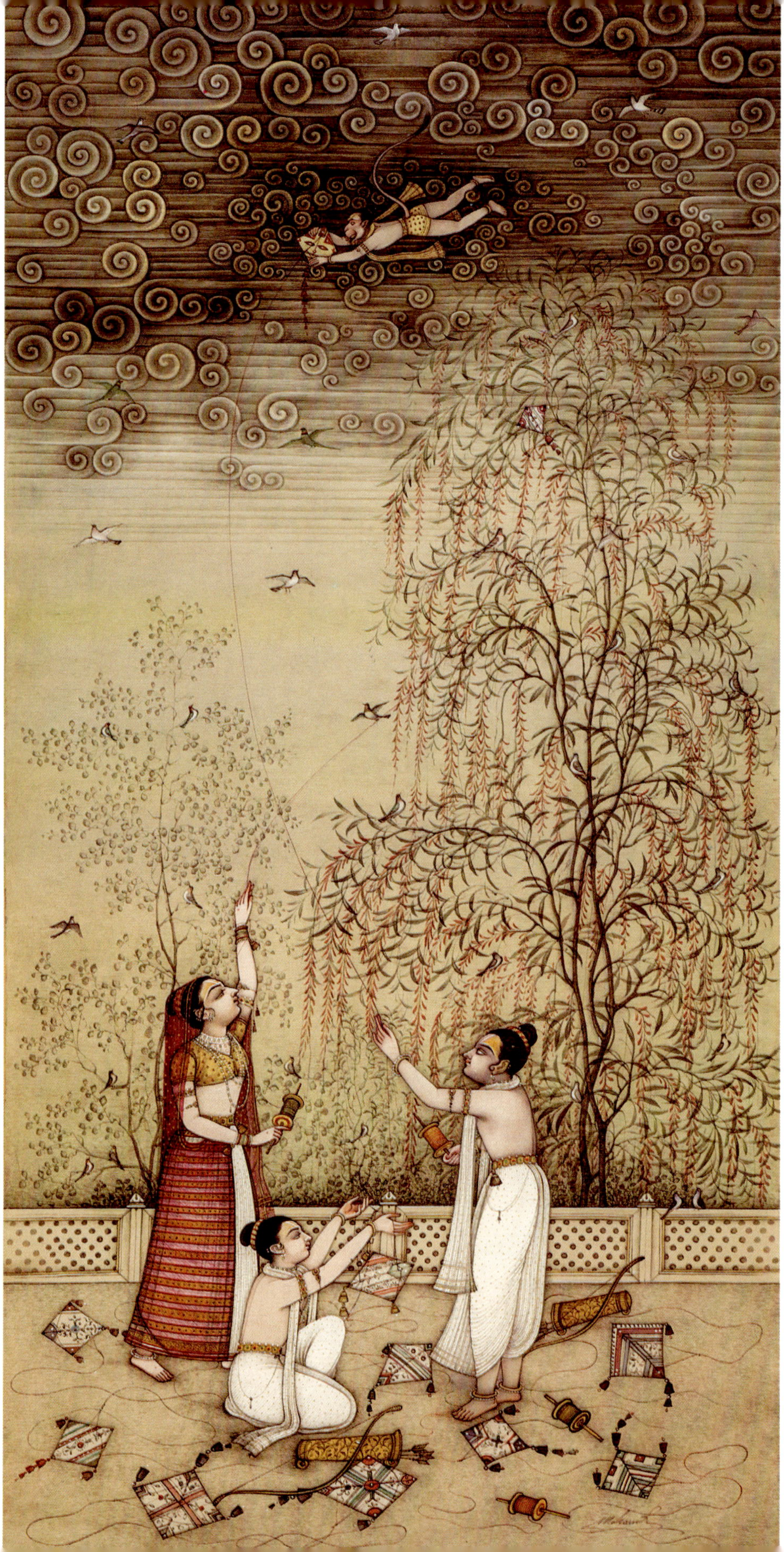

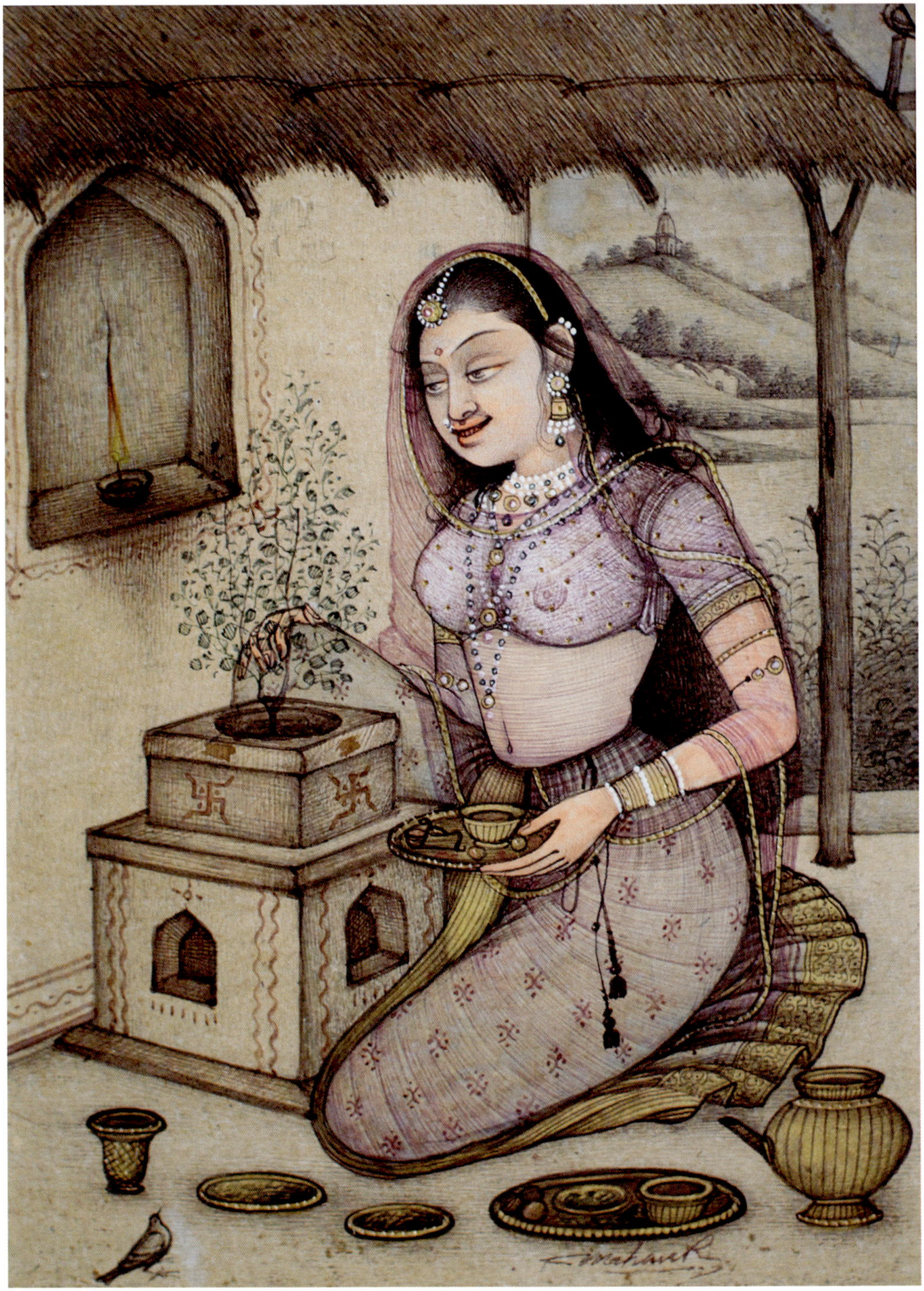

Lady worshipping Tulasi
Natural pigments on handmade paper, 15x12cm

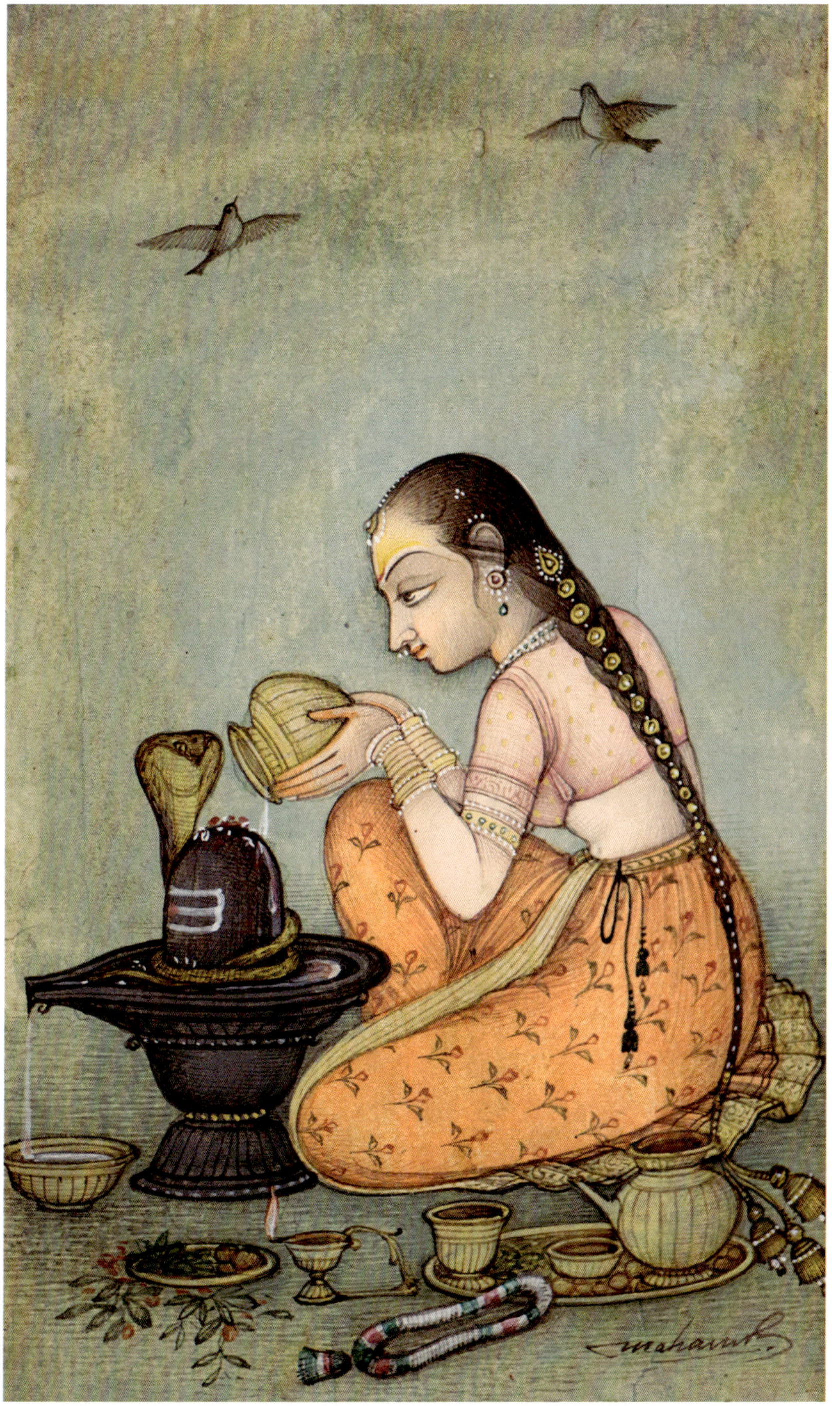

Lady worshipping Shiva linga
Natural pigments on handmade paper, 13x8cm

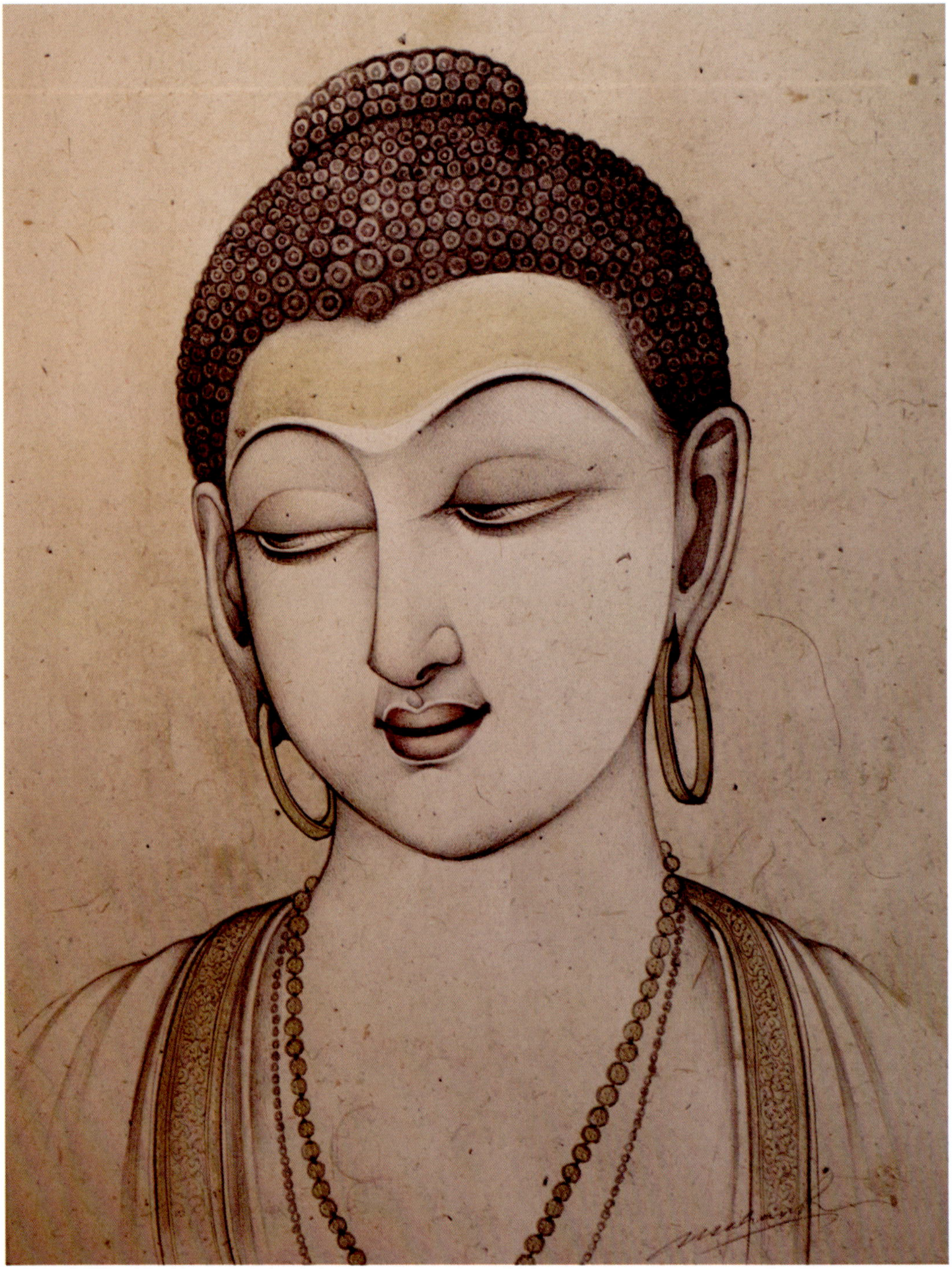

Lord Buddha
Natural pigments on handmade paper, 18x14cm

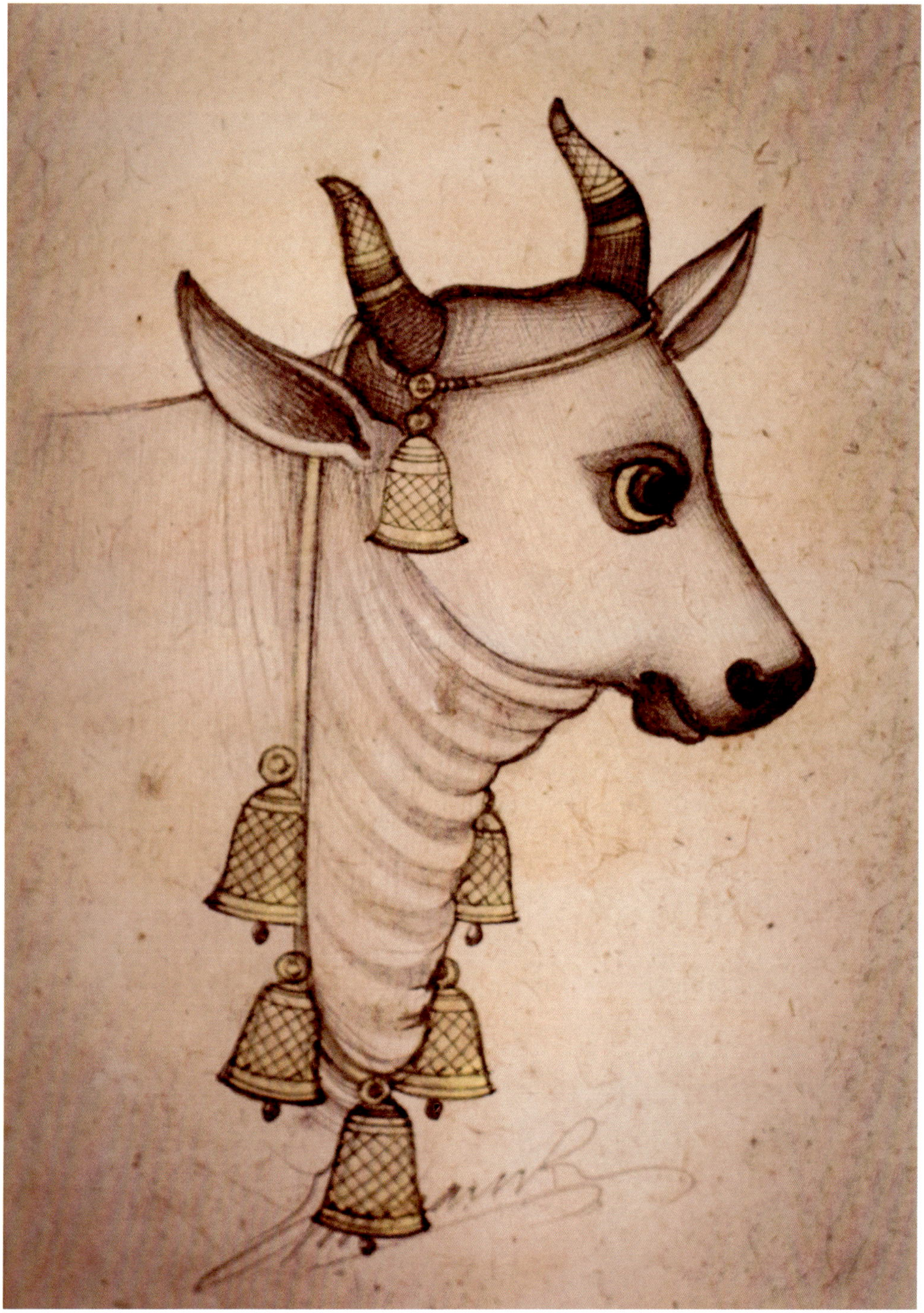

Cow
Natural pigments on handmade paper, 8x10cm

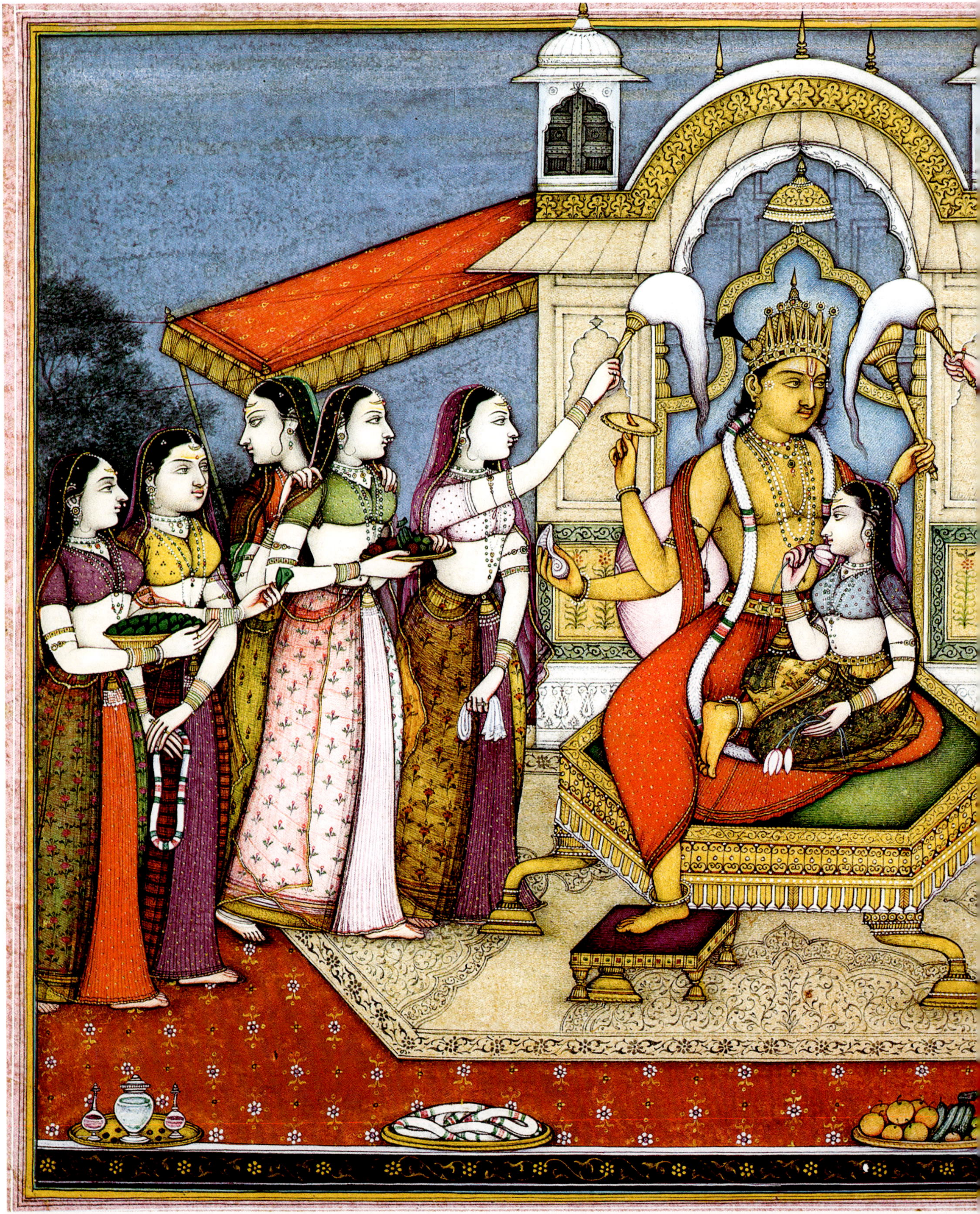

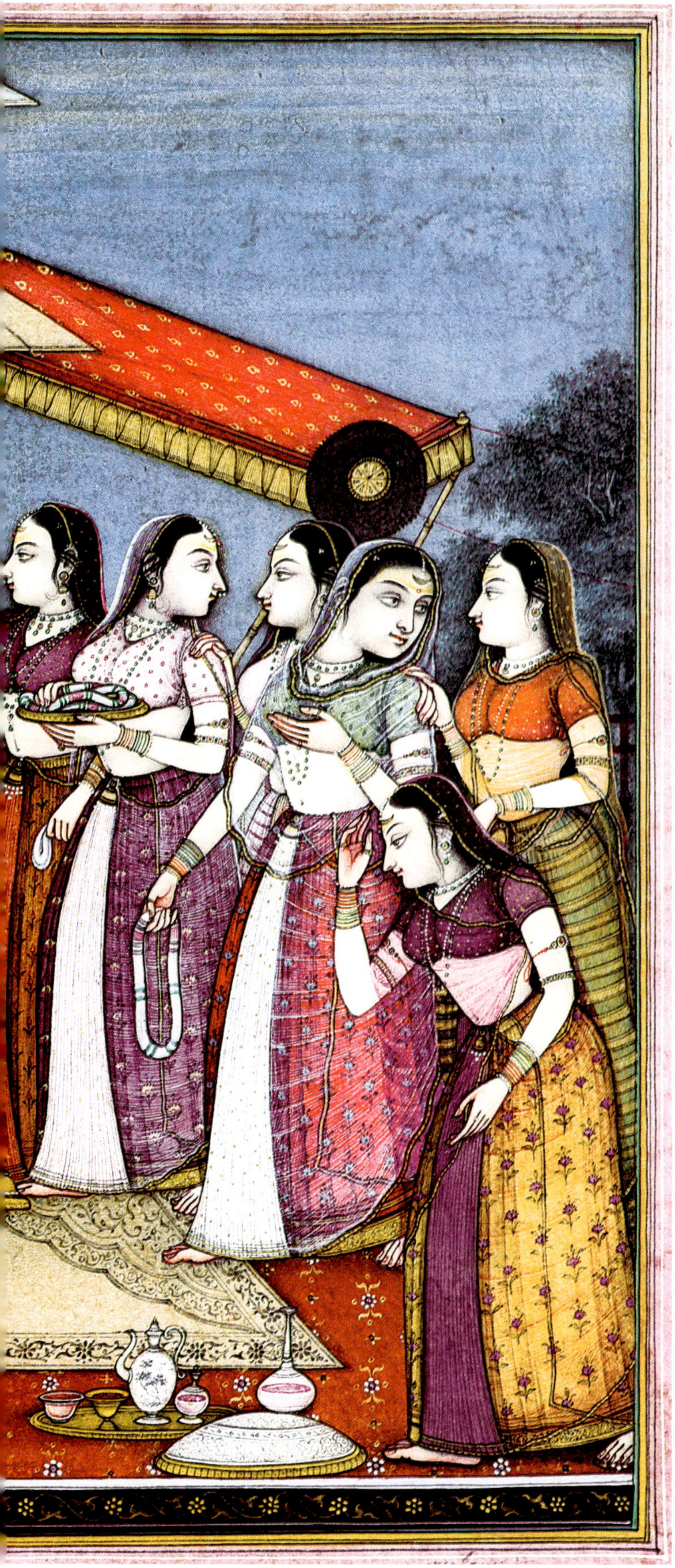

Laxmi Narayan
Natural pigments on vasli, 42x32cm

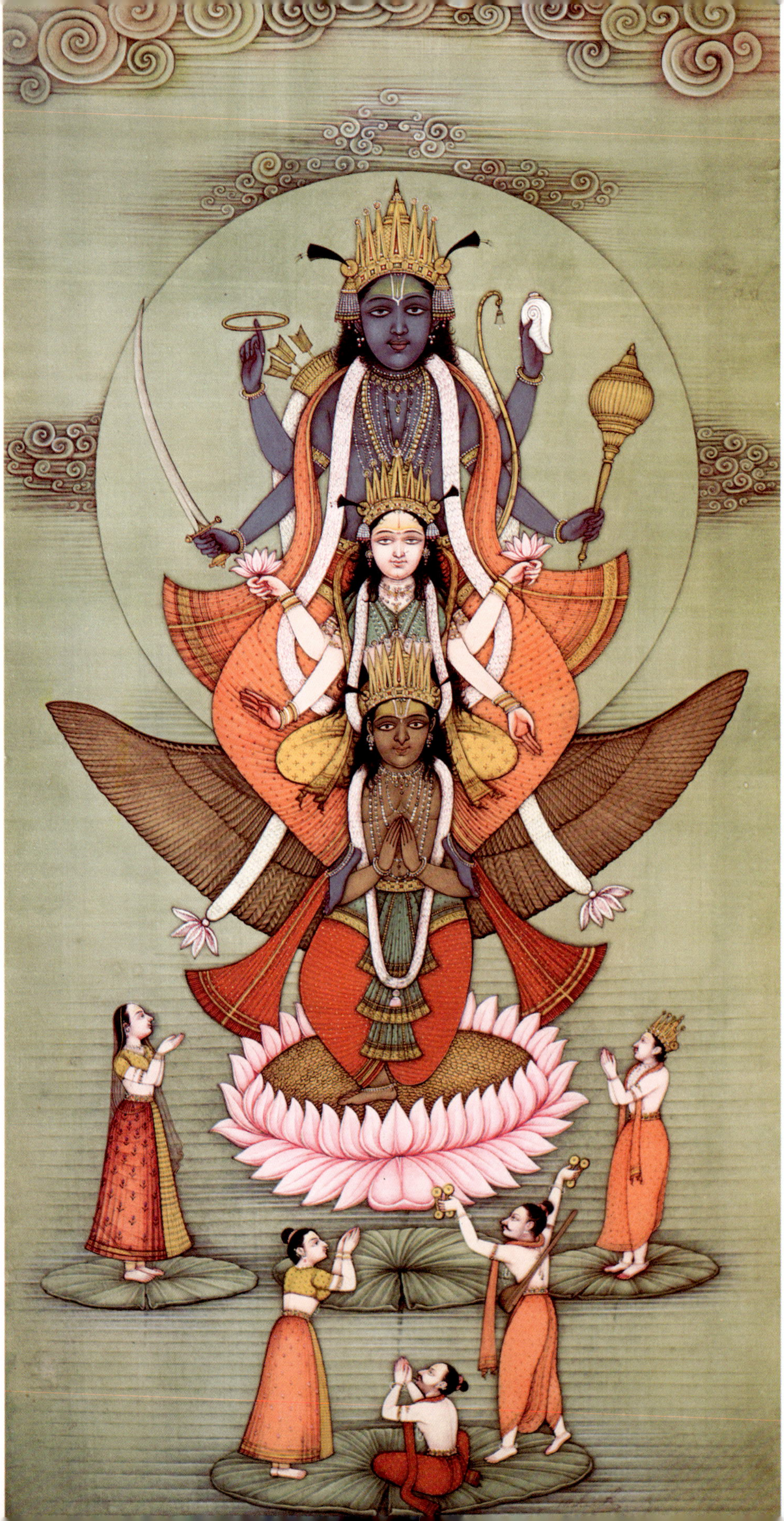

Vaibhav Laxmi
Natural pigments on
pure silk, 60x30cm

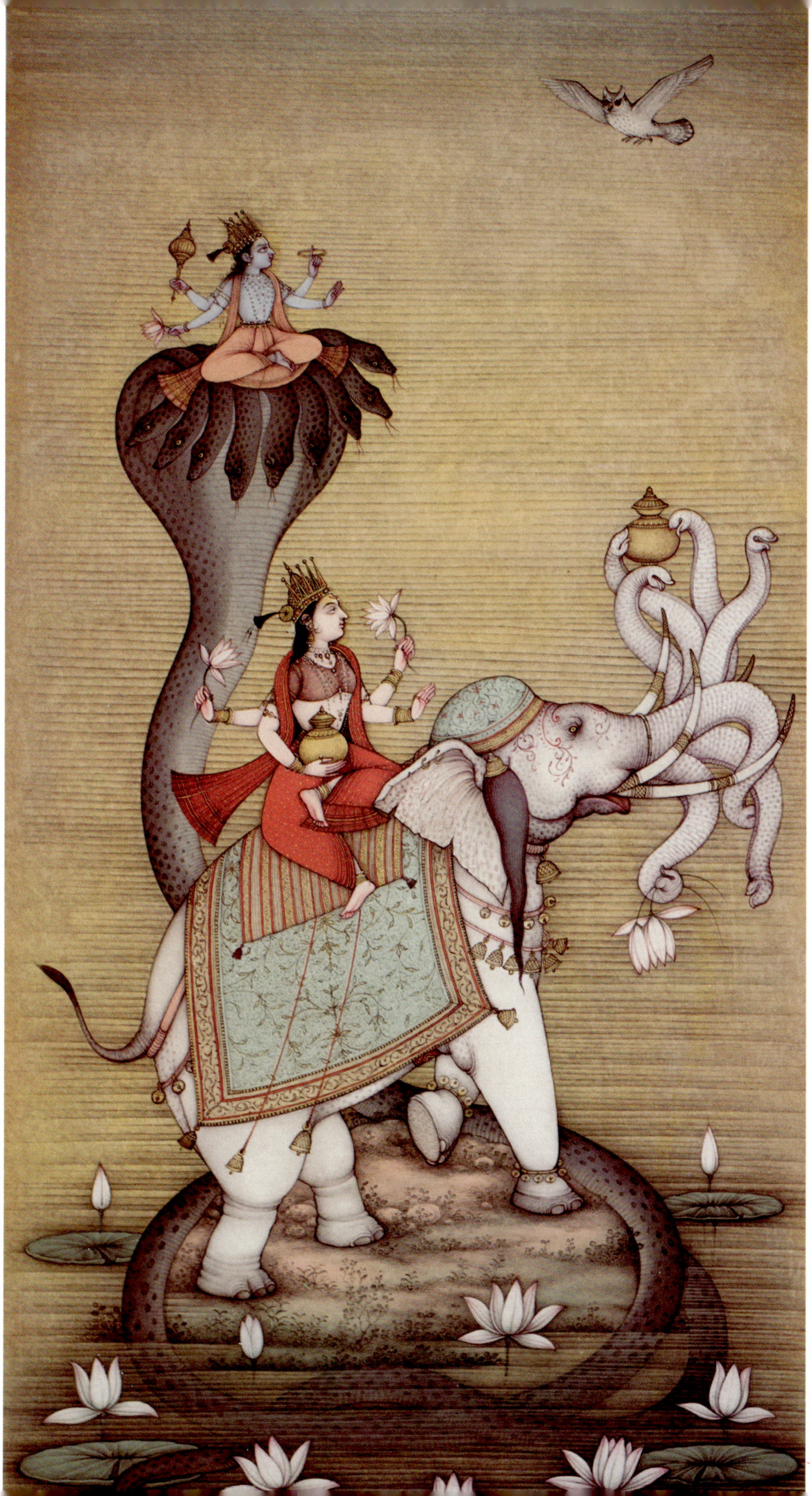

Gajendra Moksha
Natural pigments
on pure silk,
60x30cm

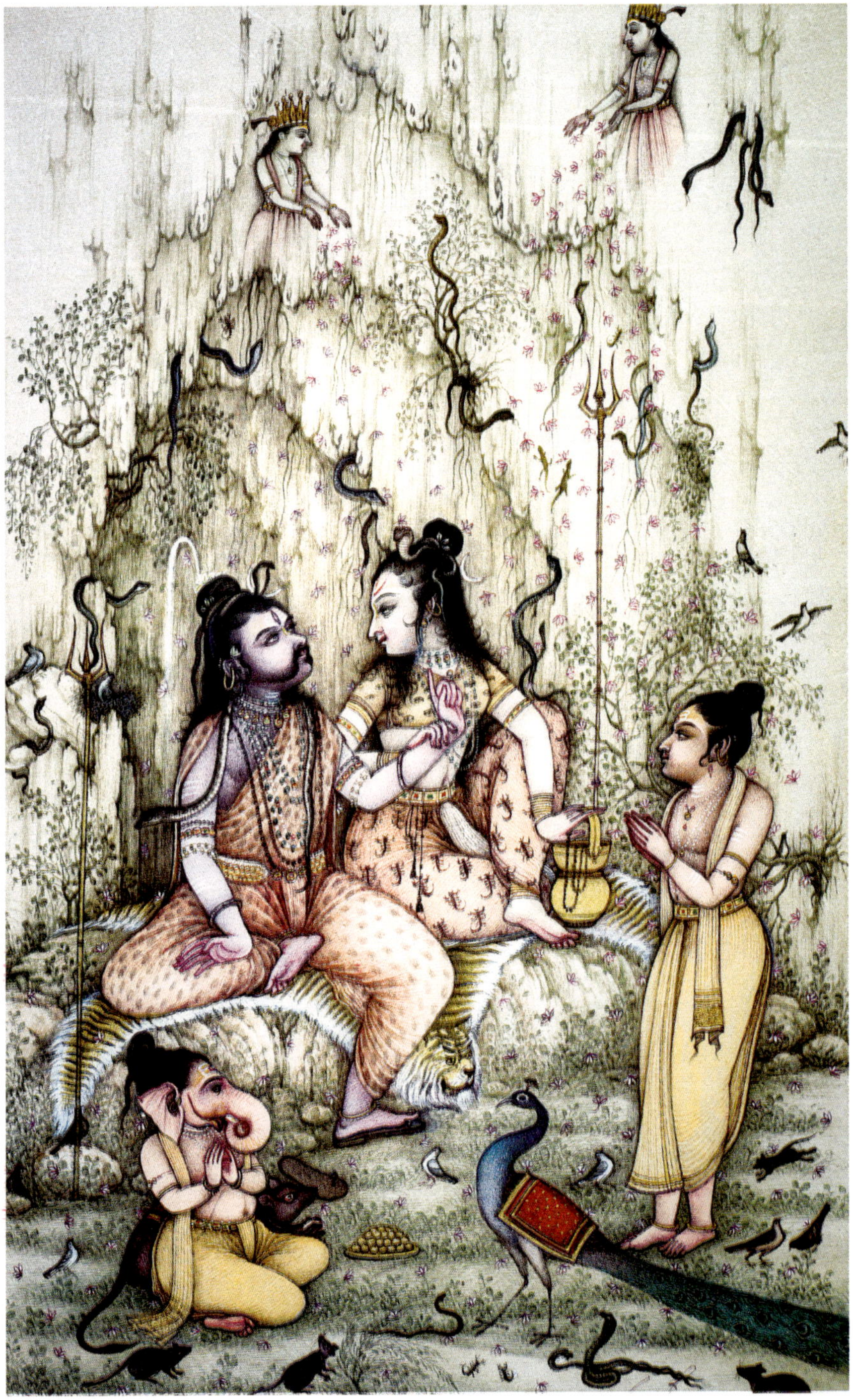

Shiv Pariwar
Natural pigments on pure silk, 27x17cm

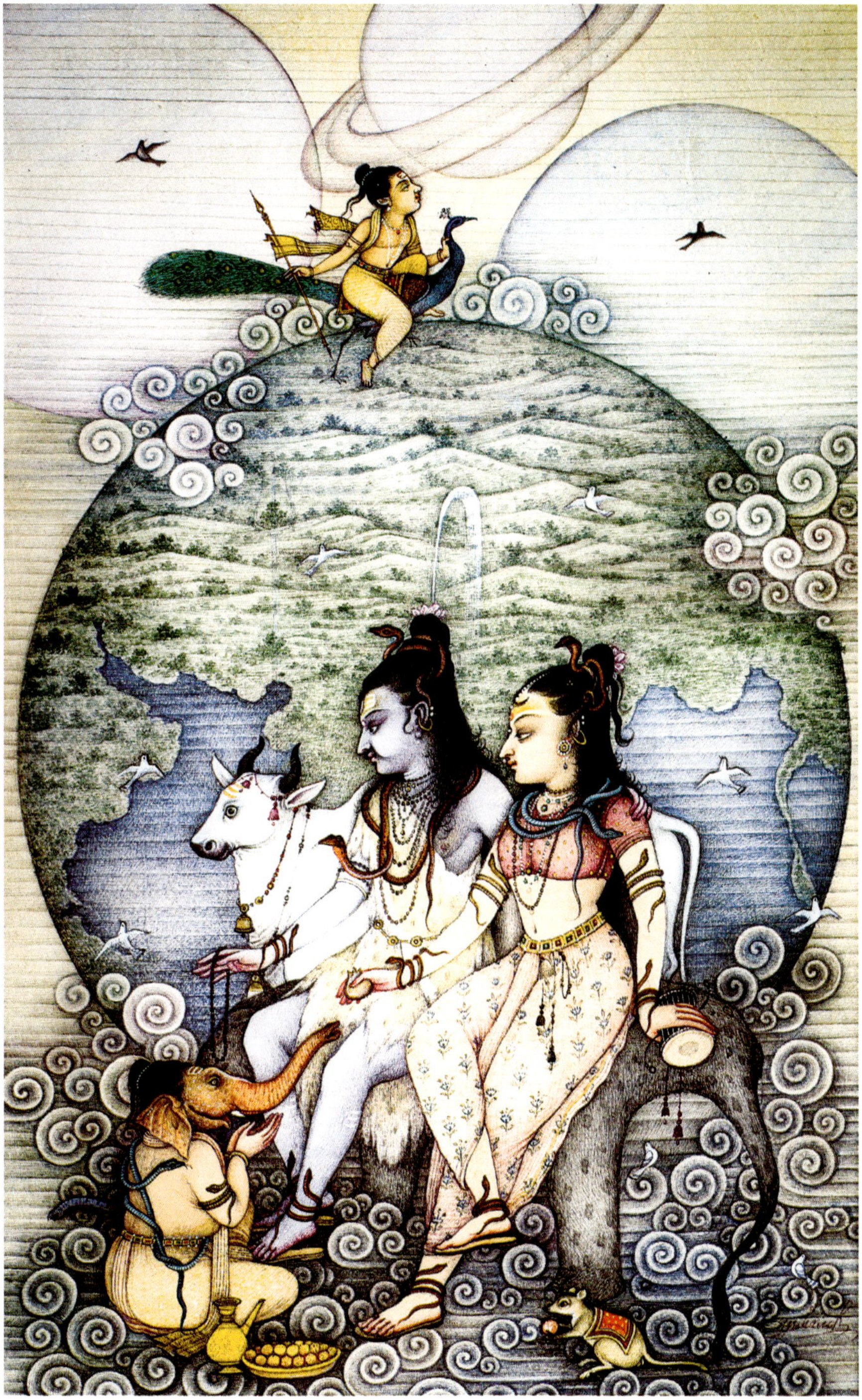

Shiv Pariwar
Natural pigments on pure silk, 27x17cm

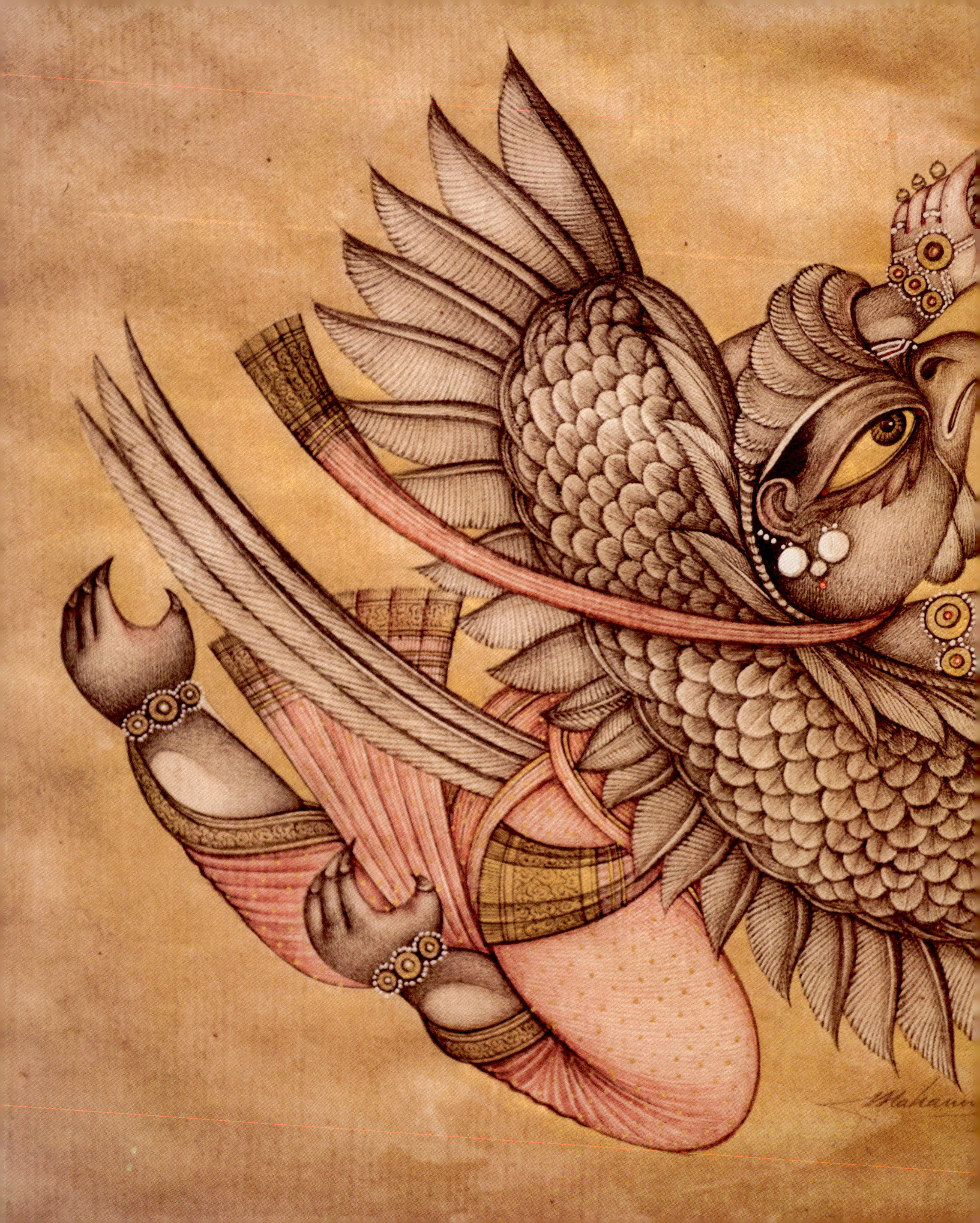

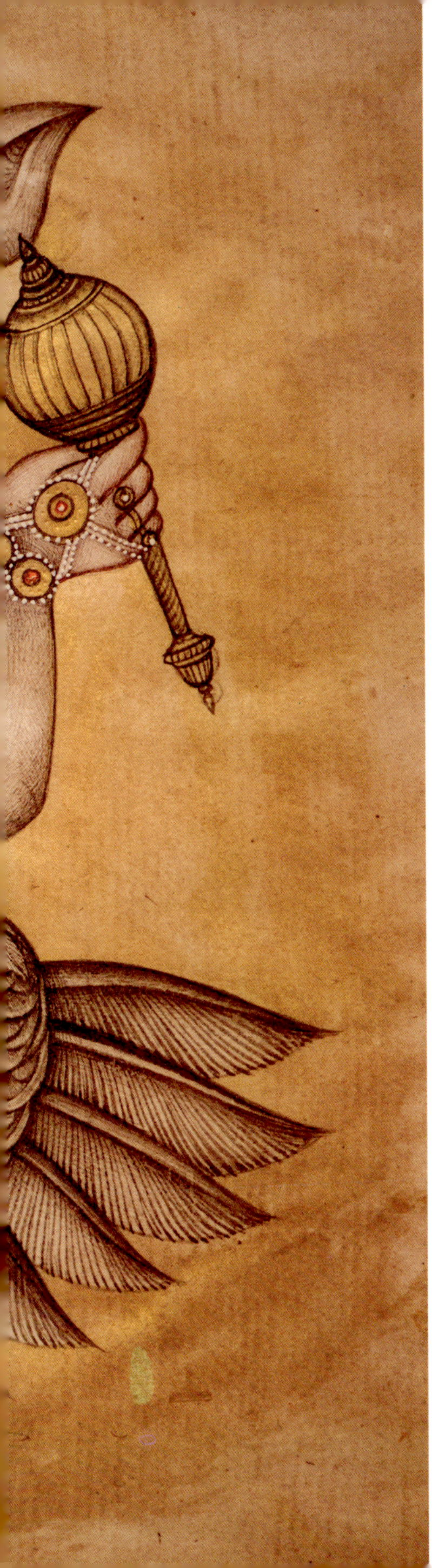

< Garuda
Natural pigments on handmade paper, 18x15cm

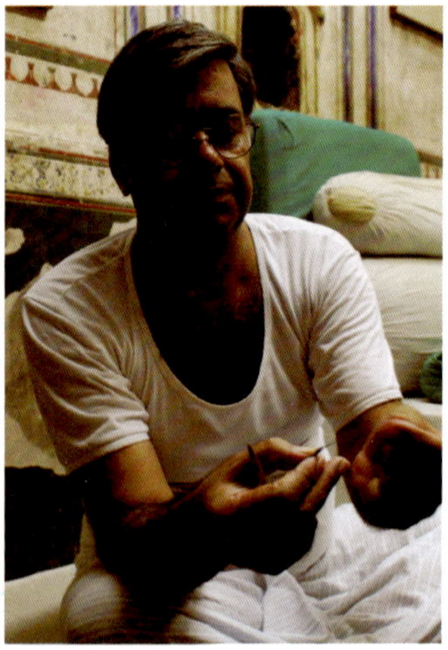

Mahaveer Swami

Born 1959 at Bikaner, Rajasthan

EDUCATION & TRAINING

1960s & 70s

Learnt mural painting from grandfather and father

1980

Passed Diploma in Painting & Sculpture, Rajasthan School of Art, Jaipur

1980-1985

Learnt miniature art under various Gurus and did commissioned work

EXHIBITIONS

1986-96

National Craft Museum, New Delhi

1988-99

Surajkund Crafts Mela, Surajkund, Haryana

1991

Galeries Lafayette, Paris

1993

Israel Arts Festival, Jerusalem

1993

Richard Kimball Art Gallery, Denver, Colorado, U.S.A.

1994

Dubai Art Festival, Dubai

1994

Galerie 88, Kolkata

1994
Private Exhibition at the Sackler Gallery, Smithsonian Institution, Washington D.C.
1994–95
Natural History Paintings from Rajasthan, Hunt Institute for Botanical Documentation, Carnegie Mellon University, Pittsburgh, Pennsylvania; and Wave Hill, New York
1995
8th International Exhibition of Botanical Art and Illustration, Hunt Institute for Botanical Documentation, Carnegie Mellon University, Pittsburgh, Pennsylvania
1995
Exhibition organized by Rajasthan Tourism Development Corporation, Bikaner
1995
World Trade Center, Mumbai, 1995
1996
Sufis, Saints & Sages, Bikaner House, New Delhi
1997
Painters & Princes, Mehrangarh Fort, Jodhpur
1997
Squirrels' Tails and Burnished Gold, Cymroza Art Gallery, Mumbai
1997
The Painters' Workshop, Mehrangarh Fort, Jodhpur
2002
Gallery J.M. Vallat, Paris
2005
Tradition & Continuity, Galerie 88, Kolkata
2005
Gallery Horikawa, Kobe, Japan
2006
Alankritha Art gallery, Hyderabad
2007
Line & Texture, Cymroza Art Gallery, Mumbai
2007
Waves Art Gallery, Pune
2007
Miniatures, Gallery Sanskriti, Kolkata
2007
Yesterday Once More: extending traditional techniques to current idioms, Apparao Galleries, Chennai

2007
Abstract Art Gallery, Bangalore
2008
From Influence To Confluence, Forty five Downstairs, Melbourne, Australia
2008
Rhythms of Brush and Pigment: Contemporary Miniatures, Ma Passion, Mumbai
2009
Harmony Art "A Tradition Revisited", Mumbai
2009
Rhythms of Brush and Pigment: Contemporary Miniatures, Ma Passion, Mumbai
2011
Elementary Botanicals, Cymroza Art Gallery, Mumbai
2011
Harvest 2011, Arushi Arts, New Delhi
2011
Rhythms of Brush and Pigment: Indian Miniatures, Ma Passion, Mumbai
2011
Hues of Tradition, Gallery Rasa, Bangalore
2012
Miniature Traditions: An Artistic Endeavour, Alankritha Art Gallery, Hyderabad
2012
Harvest 2012, Arushi Arts, New Delhi
2012
Expressions & Emotions, Arushi Arts, New Delhi
2013
Cultural Commune – Botanical Odyssey, Sudarshan Gallery, Jawahar Kala Kendra, Jaipur

AWARDS
1986
Master Craftsman Award by President of India, New Delhi
1989
Kala-Mani Award by Chief Minister of Haryana, Surajkund, Haryana
1992
Sanskriti Award by President of India, New Delhi
1995
Padam-Shree Isamudeen Ustad Award by MLA of Bikaner, Bikaner

1997

Kala-Shree Award by Chief Minister of Haryana, Surajkund, Haryana

1999

Smt. Janki Devi Somani Award, Marudhara Shodh Sansthan, Kolkata

2002

Rajiv Ratna Award, Bikaner

WORKSHOPS & CAMPS ATTENDED

1996

National Workshop on "Modern Technics and Creative Arts", Bikaner

1999

13th Surajkund Artists Camp, Surajkund, Haryana

2002-03

All India Senior Artists' Camp, AIFACS, Bikaner

2009

National Traditional and Folk Artists' Camp, Neerja Modi International School, Jaipur

2013

1st Jaipur Art Festival, Jaipur

DEMONSTRATIONS & WORKSHOPS CONDUCTED

India:

1986-96

National Craft Museum, New Delhi

1987

Department of Painting, Punjab University, Chandigarh

1988-89

Surajkund Crafts Mela, Surajkund, Haryana

1989

Kala Bhawan, Vishva Bhaarti, Santinikaten

1998

Surajkund Crafts, Haryana

1990

SAARC Festival, New Delhi

1991

Vanasthali Vidhyapeeth, Vanasthali

1991
Gwalior Trade Fair, Gwalior
1999
Marudhara Shodh Sansthan, Kolkata
Internationally:
1991 Gallery Lafayette, Paris,
1993 Israel Arts Festival, Jerusalem
1993 Egypt Museum, Cairo
1993 Dubai Art Festival, Dubai
1994 Hunt Institute for Botanical Documentation, Carnegie Mellon University, Pittsburgh, U.S.A.
1995 Freer and Sackler Art Gallery, Smithsonian Institute, Washington D.C., U.S.A.
2002 Gallery J.M. Vallat, Paris
2006 National Institute for Zorig Chusum, Thimpu, Bhutan

PAINTINGS PUBLISHED
"The Garden of Life" by Naveen Patnayak, Published by Aquarian Publishing.
"Natural history paintings from Rajasthan" by James J. White and Autumn M. Farole, Published by Hunt Institute of Botanical Documentation.

"8 International Exhibition of Botanical Art and Illustration" by James J. White, Autumn M. Farole and Sharon M. Tomasic, Published by Hunt Institute of Botanical Documentation.

"The Indian Healing Touch" by Export and Import Bank of India, Published by Mapin Publishing Private Limited.

"Aesthetic Vedanta" by Swami B.V. Tripurari, Published by Mandala Publishing Group.

"Beauty, Power and Grace" (award winner) by Krishna Dharma, Published by Mandala Publishing Group.

"Joy of Self" by B.V. Tripurari, Published by Mandala Publishing Group.

"The Bhagavad Gita: The Feeling and Philosophy" by B.V. Tripurari, Published by Mandala Publishing Group.

'From Influence to Confluence', International Gallerie (Tenth Anniversary Issue), Vol 10 No.1, 2007

Yogini: The Power of Women in Yoga, Text by Janice Gates, Illustrated by Linda Sparrow, Published by Mandala Publishing Group.

COLLECTIONS

In India

Gallery Mansur, New Delhi
Gallery 88, Kolkata
Cymroza Art Gallery, Mumbai
Sanskriti Art Gallery, Kolkata
Modi Group
Bajaj Group
Tata Group
Birla Group
Poddar Group
Seagrams Group
Arora Group
Somani Group
Ambani Group
Ma Passion Art and Heritage Corp. Ltd., Mumbai

Overseas

Rain-beau Art Gallery, Jerusalem
World Erotic Museum, Berlin
Hunt Institute Museum, Pittsburgh
Harbor Square Gallery, Camden, Maine
Sackler Art Gallery, New York
Gallery J. M. Vallat, Paris
Wave Hill Café Art Gallery, New York

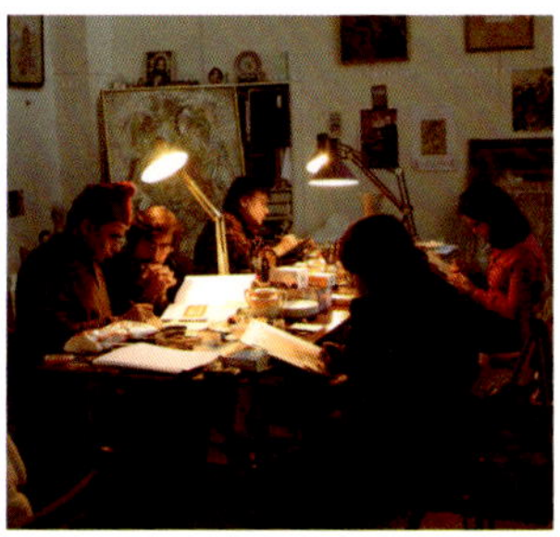

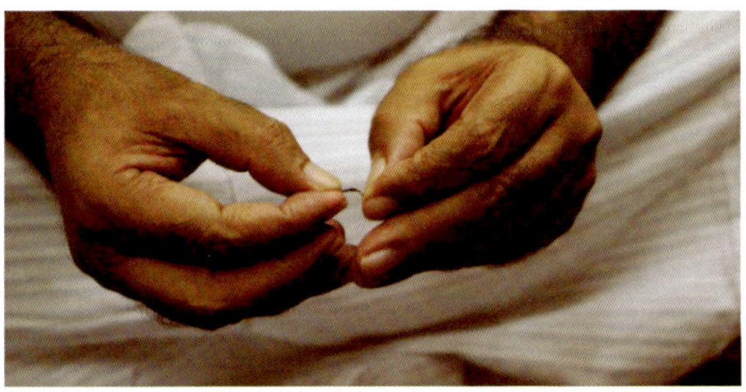

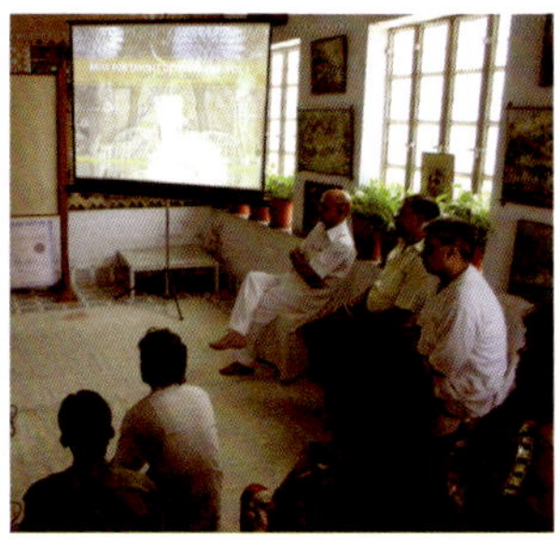